Amish Quilters

The Quilter's Son series

(4 books in one)

All scripture references in this book used from New International Version of the Bible

Table of Contents

THE QUILTER'S SON
Liam's Choice: Book 1

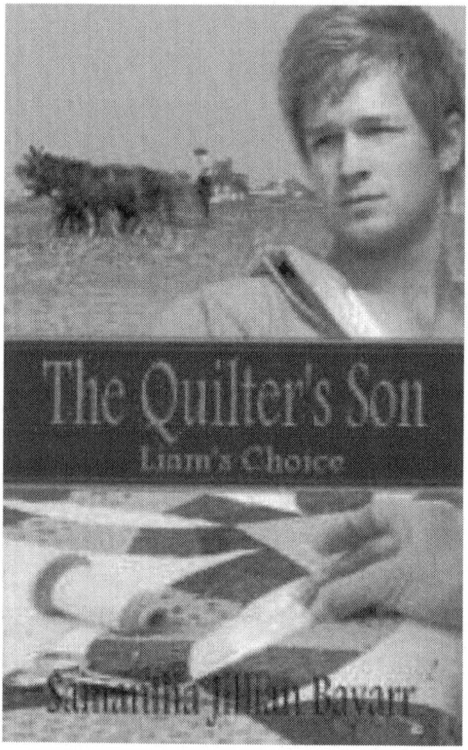

Samantha Jillian Bayarr

All scripture references in this book used from New International Version of the Bible

Chapter 1

Goshen, Indiana

"Why did you hit me?" Liam worked his jaw back and forth, the sting of the slap causing his ear to ring. But more than that, she'd crushed his spirit with one blow.

Lucy doubled her fists and planted them on her hips. She knew she would later need to take a knee and beg forgiveness, but for now, she was content with her outburst. "Did it knock any sense into you? I can give it another try if it will change your mind."

Fury showed in Lucy's eyes, her face twisted in anger. But there was something else that showed in her eyes. Fear lay just below the surface where she tried very hard to hide it.

Liam felt caught between elation that she cared so much, grief over knowing how much he would miss her when he was gone, and irritation that she would defy the commitment of peace among the Amish.

"I'm not changing my mind. You can hit me a hundred times and it won't make me stay here. I want to be on my own and explore the world. Ever since my *daed* died last month, it's made me wonder if there was more to life than what we see in our secluded little corner of this community. I feel stifled here. Computers and cell phones interest me. And I've always wanted to learn how to build more than barns. I want to design houses, and to do that, I have to learn from outside construction companies. The only opportunity I have here is plowing the same fields my *daed* did his entire life. I want more out of life than that, and my *daed* knew that. When I die, I want my life to mean something."

Lucy looked at him through the veil of tears that blurred her vision. "You really think your *daed's* life amounted to nothing?"

"*Mei daed* knew I didn't want to be a farmer. That's why he let me go to the public school behind my *mamm's* back. With only three weeks left of my senior year after he died, I continued to go so I could graduate because I'm more determined than ever to get out of this backward society."

Lucy's lips formed a grim line, and tears spilled from her eyes. "If you think being Amish is *backward,* then perhaps you're correct in saying you don't belong here. But at least have the decency to face your *mamm* instead of sneaking out the window this late at night."

Liam kicked at the knapsack that rested against the large oak tree that stood beside the *haus*. It was almost too dark to see the expression on Lucy's face, but what he saw of it, he didn't like. "You didn't complain any of those nights I snuck out the window to meet with you."

"That's because I thought you had intended to marry me. Now I find out you stole that first kiss from me that I was saving for my husband; I can never get that back."

Liam braced his hands on her forearms. "Then come with me. We can still get married. We can get a little apartment and live in the city."

Lucy broke from his grasp, her face curling with disgust. "I could never get married without my *familye.* And I won't marry a *mann* who isn't baptized."

Liam picked up his knapsack and flung the weight of it over one shoulder. "Then I suppose we will be parting ways. If I take the baptism I will be destined to be just like my *daed.*"

Lucy sobbed. "Would that really be so bad? How do you think he would feel if he could see you now running away from your *familye* like a coward?"

Liam yanked the straw hat from his head and tossed it to the ground. "He isn't here. My *mamm* and *schweschder* will be better off without me. As long as I don't want to be here, my heart isn't in it. So what's the point in staying? So I can make them as miserable as I am? Besides, Lydia no longer talks to me, and *mamm* doesn't talk to either of us. All she does is sit at her quilting frame and sew quilts. Neither of them will even notice I'm gone."

Lucy sniffled, closing the space between them.

"Even if they don't, I will."

Liam backed away from her. If he kissed her now, he would never have the courage to leave. He didn't want things to end between them; he loved her a great deal, but he guessed it wasn't enough to make him want to stay. If he changed his mind it wouldn't be because of the opinion or request of another person. He had to stay for himself, and that wasn't how he felt. His desire to go was too strong to let anything or anyone get in his way—even if that meant he would have to break the heart of the woman he loved.

Lucy found it difficult to breathe. How could Liam do this to his *familye*—to her? Suddenly all the excuses he'd given her over the past few years regarding his busyness had made sense. He was too busy because he'd been leading a double life. Going to school all day and then working his chores around such a demanding schedule. Was he leaving her because he didn't think she was smart enough for him? Did he want someone better than her?

"Will you at least give it some more thought? Have you even prayed about it?"

Liam looked away. He hadn't prayed about it in the past month. He hadn't reached out to *Gott* about much since his *daed* died. He didn't want to hear the answer his heart was nudging him toward. He'd had his mind made up for some time, and now that he was eighteen, it was time.

Lucy nodded. "Your silence tells me you haven't prayed. Since you are so determined to abandon your *familye* and your faith, will you at least tell me where you're going so I can visit you?"

Liam paused. "*Nee,* it will be too far. I'm heading toward Michigan."

He didn't tell her that he was too nervous to go too far. Most likely, he would stay in Indiana and go to South Bend where his friends planned on renting a small house. He feared that if Lucy knew he would be living only a few miles away, she would constantly nag him about returning home.

Lucy lifted her chin in defiance. "If you're determined to go, then don't come back because I won't be waiting for you."

Her statement hurt worse than the slap she'd delivered across his face just a few moments earlier. Liam watched his future walk away from him, as he told himself a better future waited for him in the next town over. They'd both made their decision, and now they would have to live with it. Liam was confident he had his *daed's* blessing to leave, and that was all that mattered at the moment.

Chapter 2

South Bend, Indiana

"I still look Amish," Liam complained as he studied his appearance in the dressing room mirror.

"I'm going to need a haircut."

He had chosen the clothing store in the mall, after his new roommate, Steve, advised him that the store carried the latest styles. He liked the casual look of the sweatshirt and jeans, but his hair still gave him away. A quick stop at the barber shop would get rid of all traces of the Amish in him. But it couldn't erase the pull he still felt in his heart. At eighteen, his biggest desire was to stay as far away from the Amish community as possible, and leave the pain of losing his *daed* behind him once and for all.

His *mamm* had no idea he'd been sneaking away to the public school for the past four years to get his diploma. His *daed* had helped him hide it from his *mamm,* but after the accident, his *mamm* was too consumed with grief to even notice Liam's antics when he continued to go. His twin sister, Lydia, was too busy caring for the house and doing all the things their *mamm* used to do before the buggy accident that took their father's life, so she hadn't noticed either.

It was a tough time for everyone, and Liam was responsible for the upkeep of the farm. Spending all day in school and keeping up with his studies was difficult to do with a farm to maintain, but he'd been determined to leave home and start a new life for himself, leaving Lydia to take over in his absence.

He was now finished with his senior year and needed the diploma to get a job out in the *real world,* as he'd come to know it. His friends at school had guided him every step of the way, right down to teaching him how to drive a car and how to dress and act so he could hide his heritage from the outside world. The transition had not been an easy one, but it was what he felt he needed to do to stifle the grief he still held onto over his father's death.

Liam's refusal of the Bishop's prompting to receive the baptism to seal his Amish roots had not gone over well with anyone. He felt guilty for leaving his *mamm* and *schweschder*, but he didn't see his leaving would change things much. He'd been a coward and left his *mamm* a note letting her know he was leaving, but he didn't think about how it would affect her. His being there had gone unnoticed when his family stopped functioning after his *daed's* accident.

Liam determinedly put the memories behind him, unable to imagine the regret that would hound him over the next few years…

Chapter 3

Seven years later…

A summer breeze rustled the leaves on the trees in front of the shops that lined Main Street in Goshen. Being a typical July morning in Indiana, steamy mist rose from the dew-drenched patches of grass that lined the walkways as the sun warmed up the earth. Liam stood across the street behind a maple tree, hoping his mother and his sister would not notice him watching them. He knew the nature of the Amish was to walk with downcast eyes when in public because he'd spent the first eighteen years of his life doing the same, but he feared his mother would somehow sense his presence and look his way. Since he'd left home, he'd grown into a man—an *Englischer.* But that wouldn't stop a mother from recognizing her own son, would it?

When his mother and sister entered the small quilt shop, he noticed his mother had used a key to open the door. He knew the insurance company of the driver of the car that had killed his father had presented his mother with a sizable settlement, and he wondered now if she'd finally used it to open the shop. Part of him wanted to go to her and ease the worry lines that creased her aging face, but too much time had passed. A reunion would only open old wounds. Since he hadn't taken the baptism, his actions had not earned him a shunning, but that wouldn't keep his family from turning a cold shoulder to him—something he felt he deserved.

Even if he were to approach them, he knew he couldn't handle the pain of rejection from his own mother and sister. Shame crept into his heart for his act of betrayal toward his family and the community. He felt like a coward, and he had to admit that his life away from them had been empty and lonely. He'd thrown himself into his work, earning enough money working for others to start his own business. Now with seven men that counted on him, he felt the strain even more.

They'd only had a few big jobs so far this year, and if he didn't bring in more work soon, his company would perish, along with all his hard work. But what had it all been for? To escape a community shunned by the outside world, only to trade it for being shunned by the people he loved most? Now, as he stood across the street watching his mother and sister enter *The Quilter's Square,* Liam suddenly questioned the decision he'd made seven long years ago…

Nellie Yoder felt a breeze brush by her, and with it came the feeling she was being watched. Out of the corner of her eye, she spotted the *Englischer* again; he was standing across the street as if waiting for an invitation from her. She felt his presence, the same as if she were still carrying him in her womb. After all, a mother knows her own flesh and blood. She had managed to swallow the lump that formed in her throat and compose herself for the sake of the *dochder* who had not left her side during the years since her husband's death. Nellie longed to hold her son and tell him how much he'd been missed, but only time would tell if such a dream could become reality.

She ushered Lydia into the quilt shop before the girl noticed her twin brother loitering across the street. What had she been thinking when she'd opened this shop? She knew that it needed repairs that she couldn't fix on her own. She'd known about Liam's business for several months, and thought it would give her the opportunity to bring her son home where he belonged. Her plan was to hire him to do the renovations, hoping it would draw him back to his *familye* and the community.

Now, as she saw him for the third day in a row, Nellie suddenly wondered if she should have thought things through a little more clearly. After all these years of letting her husband's settlement sit idle, she wondered if using it to get her son back was the wisest thing she could have done. She feared that because so much time had passed, he would be more resistant to returning to the community. But after seeing him watching her again this morning, she was convinced she'd made the right move. She knew she would have to proceed with caution, so as not to upset Lydia or spook Liam. She didn't want him to run from her, but so far, he'd not approached her either. She sighed deeply as she watched him walk away, knowing it was too late to abandon her plan now. The first step had already been taken.

Chapter 4

Lydia tried not to alert her *mamm*, who hadn't seemed to notice her own son standing across the street watching them for the third day this week. The urge to talk to her estranged twin outweighed any fear of getting her heart broken again if he should turn his back on them all over again. Her heart ached to run to him and talk to him like they hadn't since they were mere children on the farm—before the tragedy that tore their *familye* apart, and before Liam left them to fend for themselves.

Lydia felt a mixture of anger and love for her *bruder*, if that was possible. She knew that approaching him would put her and her *mamm* at risk of being reprimanded by the Bishop, but she wasn't sure she cared at this point. Too much time had been lost, and too much suffering had consumed their *familye* already.

Guilt crept back into her heart as she momentarily replayed the day her *bruder* left them. For years, she'd wondered if her harsh words had pushed Liam further into his decision to leave. She'd discovered he'd been attending the public school, and had scolded him for thinking only of himself. That day he'd asked her to attend his high school graduation, and she'd refused. She'd accused him of being selfish and had told him to leave. She hadn't meant it, and she'd regretted those words ever since that day.

Even now, no matter how much her love for her *bruder* tugged at Lydia's heart, logic reminded her how difficult life would be for her *mamm* if she were to get her hopes up regarding her son's return to the community—especially if he rejected them again. Lydia had been the one who'd stayed, but she hadn't taken the baptism. She'd remained with their *mamm* all these years and shouldered the responsibility on her own.

For weeks after Liam ran off, Lydia had waited for him to return, hoping that he would get a taste of the outside world but that it would be so difficult he would return home. When weeks turned to months, and months turned to years, hope for such a miracle had nearly dwindled to nothing—until three days ago.

Lucy Graber watched out the bay window of her bakery front as she stacked cookies and pastries in the display case under the counter that ran the length of the store. For three days now, she'd watched the handsome stranger linger across the street in the early morning hours.

There was a familiarity about him that she couldn't quite push aside. She had all but convinced herself that the *Englischer* was Liam Yoder, but she didn't dare hope for such a foolish thing. She had given up hope of his return too many years ago to count. Before his *daed* died, the two of them had been seeing one another secretly, and even though their love was still fairly new, Lucy had been convinced she would marry him one day. Within days after the tragedy struck his *familye*, Liam began to pull away from Lucy. They'd shared their first and last kiss in the early morning hours before the accident that had taken the life of Liam's *daed*. Lucy had felt Liam's promise in that kiss—a promise that would never come to pass.

Liam hung his head as he walked down the street toward his work truck. He hadn't realized just how much his heart ached from the separation from his family until seeing them again. But he felt too much shame to approach them. He was supposed to go into town with his father the morning of the accident. Instead, he'd been out too late with Lucy, and had fallen asleep in the barn after chores. He vaguely remembered his dad finding him in the hayloft and telling him to stay put, that he would run the errands in town alone. He'd never been able to shake the guilt of allowing his dad to go without him. Guilt had overcome Liam knowing that if only he'd been with his father, he could have done something to save his life that morning. His lack of responsibility that day had destroyed his family and cost him a future with Lucy.

When his cell phone rang, Liam pulled it from his back pocket and held it to his ear.

"Hey boss," Steve said. "You on your way in? We got a call for a new job this morning. We're expected on the site in two hours to give an estimate. Sounds like a big one."

The news of a job lifted Liam's spirits. "I'm on my way."

He hung up the phone and looked back toward the quilting shop one last time before hopping into his truck and driving away.

Chapter 5

Liam's heart did a flip-flop against his chest wall when Steve showed him the name of the shop owner that was requesting an estimate. How could he go to his mother's shop and mingle with his family when they probably didn't have any desire to talk to him since he'd forsaken them? There were two Yoder's Construction companies in the area; why had his mother chosen his? Was it the name she trusted, or had she known it was his company when she'd made the call? The other Yoder Construction was closer to them as it was in Goshen, but the majority of their work was building houses from start to finish, while Liam and his crew did mostly repair and reconstructive work out of South Bend. He'd always hoped he could build houses, but things just hadn't turned out that way.

"Why don't you take this one, Steve? I have a possible job on the other side of town to check on. It's another small one, but at least it's honest work."

Liam was suddenly grateful that he'd taken the call about the other job on the way back to his office.

Though he had first intended on sending Steve to get the estimate for the smaller job across town, his only focus now was delaying an awkward reunion with his family. Getting the estimate for his mother had changed everything.

"Are you sure, Boss? This is a pretty big job and I don't want to give the wrong figures."

Liam patted his friend on the back. "You have to learn sometime, Steve. Besides, I trust you to bring all the particulars back to the office so we can go over it before giving the shop owner a final estimate."

Liam wasn't sure how he would handle the job if they took it, but he also couldn't leave his family to work with another contractor that might not do the job as well as he would. He cringed at the thought of someone taking advantage of his mother and charging her too much for less than perfect work. His own skills were by no means perfected, but he knew his mother and what would make her happy—at least he used to.

Liam paced the length of his office until he heard Steve's truck pull into the parking lot. What had taken the man so long to get the estimate from his mother? Had she told Steve she was his *mamm?* Steve had known he'd grown up Amish, but Liam had never told any of the guys he worked with about his past. It had never come up, and Liam never felt comfortable sharing anything so private with any of them. As far as they knew, he was their boss, and that was good enough for them. Aside from a few of the guys sharing that their wives nagged them to come home early all the time, none of them ever openly shared anything too personal about their lives, and that was how Liam preferred it.

Steve entered the office and put his clipboard down on Liam's desk with a huff.

"Whoever sold that woman the property ought to be ashamed of himself. The plumbing and electrical all needs to be updated and up to code. The ceiling has holes and rotted tiles from a leak somewhere. And the walls are rotted and crumbling. The place looks like there was a fire."

If memory served him, Liam recalled a fire that had consumed several of the shops in the downtown district a couple of years back, but nearly all of them had been renovated since then. The outside sign looked outdated—probably belonging to the previous owner. But if he knew his *mamm* as much he thought he did, she would have taken it literally as a sign she was meant to have the shop—no matter what condition it was in. Had she planned to hire him from the time she'd signed the papers of ownership on the place? His mother was too smart to be sold a dilapidated property—unless she had other plans for it. Plans that involved him.

Nellie was a little more than disappointed that her own son had sent one of his employees to take the assessment of her repairs. The *mann* had told her he would need to take them back to the office to consult with his boss before giving a full estimate. She'd hoped to finally see her son face-to-face, but it seemed *Gott* had other plans for her today.

After being pointed out all the faults the shop held, she was confident it would be enough to keep Liam and his crew around long enough for her to repair her relationship with him while he repaired her shop. She prayed he wasn't avoiding her by not coming to give the estimate, but perhaps it was not something he did on a regular basis. After all, her son was the boss—of his own company. Nellie couldn't be more proud, unless he chose to return to the Amish ways. But that was a prayer for another day.

Lydia watched her *mamm's* face fall when the young *mann* walked into the shop wearing a blue shirt with the name *Yoder Construction* embroidered on the pocket. She wondered if her *mamm* knew it was Liam's company, and she'd hoped he would show up. Unsure of her *mamm's* source of disappointment, she didn't dare bring up her *bruder* in case her *mamm* didn't know about him just yet. She would soon enough, and they would deal with it then—together—as a *familye.*

Lucy balanced the plate of cookies in one hand and a pitcher of iced tea in the other, three paper cups tucked under her arm as she entered Nellie's quilt shop.

Nellie looked up as the door squeaked open and her neighbor entered.

Lucy smiled. "I thought you might want some refreshment. It's such a warm day today."

Nellie approached the young girl and took the tea and cups from her, setting them down on a table she'd brought from the farm. "*Danki.* This place is going to need more work than I originally thought. It seems it needs more than just a thorough cleaning."

Lucy looked around. "I was lucky *mei daed* had my shop cleaned and fixed before he gave it to me for my eighteenth birthday. I think he decided I might as well have something to fall back on since it wasn't likely I'd be taking a husband. He was right because here I am seven years later, and still without a husband."

Nellie felt sorry for Lucy. She knew that she was sweet on her only son, and it broke her heart that the two of them weren't giving her any *grandkinner.*

"Don't give up hope, dear Lucy. You never know what *Gott* has waiting for you just around the corner. You're still young. You shouldn't give up hope. He could bless you when least you expect it."

Lucy hoped the woman was right. Was it too late to hope that Liam would come back to her?

Chapter 6

"But Boss," Steve protested. "Don't you think you should let Henry go do the smaller job so you can come with me and rest of the guys to the big job? I know you're the boss, but this will be our *biggest* job this year."

Liam shook his head. "I can finish painting the house in three days, tops. Those first few days at the quilt shop will be spent assessing, measuring, and making a list of all the supplies needed. By the time I finish at the other place, you'll be ready to start this one. I have faith in you. Besides, Henry has more experience than I do with this stuff. But I'll expect a full report at the end of each day."

Steve tipped his cap toward Liam. "You're the boss."

Liam managed a half-smile. "That's what they tell me."

He knew he would eventually have to show up at his mother's quilt shop to do the job she'd hired his company to do, but a few days would give him enough time to prepare for their first meeting after so many years apart. It wouldn't be easy seeing her again, and Liam hoped she wouldn't fire him and his men when she discovered who it was she'd actually hired.

Liam grabbed a cup of coffee for the road and headed toward the paint job, while his crew went the opposite direction to his mother's quilt shop. His heart ached to see his family again, but he just wasn't ready yet. He hadn't realized just how much he'd missed them until he'd seen them quite by accident that first day outside of the quilt shop.

Liam had actually been on his way into the bakery next door to the quilt shop that first morning when he'd happened upon his mother and sister. After hearing from Steve about a pastry he'd purchased at the bakery that tasted like Christmas, he knew he had to check it out. He'd only known of one person in his life that could make the sort of pastry his employee had described, and he'd had to see for himself if what he suspected was true. When he happened upon his mother and sister that morning instead, thoughts of Lucy Graber and her pastries had left his mind—until now.

Liam couldn't be sure what it was that triggered the memory of Lucy, but perhaps it was the roses that bordered the porch of the house he was about to paint. He used to pick roses from his mother's garden and bring them to Lucy when they would steal away late after dark to spend a few moments together when they were young.

She'd always allowed the sweetest little giggle to escape her lips whenever he would bring her roses. Then her cheeks would flame from the embarrassment. Liam had thought she was the prettiest girl he'd ever seen. But Lucy was surely married by now with several *kinner;* he was certain of it. There was no sense in going to the bakery only to be disappointed when he wasn't certain he would find her there. But if he'd known she was possibly working just a few miles from where he'd been living, he'd have gone to see her long before this.

Liam's biggest problem now was how to handle the meeting with his mother and sister while his employees stood by and watched. He hadn't told any of them of his past, with the exception of Steve, who'd gone to school with him. But the two of them had buried that secret a long time ago. He hoped his employees wouldn't think any differently of him if they were to find out his secret. After all, everyone has a past. If any of them would be accepting, Henry would be the most understanding. After spending several years in jail for stealing building supplies from his former employer, he was grateful for Liam's ability to overlook his past. Given the older man's past history, he was lucky to have a job, and he was very much aware of that fact. Liam had been the only construction company to give the man a chance, and he was glad he had. Not only was Henry a hard worker, he taught Liam things that improved his skills as a contractor.

Wiping the sweat from his brow, Liam considered holding a meeting with his staff as he prepped the house for painting. He'd spent the past hour scraping chips of old paint from the backside of the house, and now he was ready to begin painting. The wood siding was weather-worn, but luckily, the back was the only side that had begun to chip and peel.

If I held a meeting, what would I say to them? Maybe it would be better if I just wing it. If they're caught off guard, they may let it go and not say anything in front of my familye. But there's always the chance either my mamm or my schweschder will not even speak to me.

Chapter 7

Nellie continued to scrub the floors of her new quilt shop while the *menner* from her son's company took measurements and wrote things on clipboards. So far her plan to spend time with Liam had backfired on her. She was more than disappointed when he didn't show up with the others, but her ears perked up when she overheard one of the *menner* say that Liam was at another job for the next few days. By the end of the week, she would be reunited with her son.

In some ways, she was grateful for the extra time, hoping that when he did show up he wouldn't take his *menner* and leave since they'd already begun the job for her. Nellie felt the timing was to her advantage, and so she determined to be patient for her long-awaited meeting with her only son. She wondered how her *dochder* would react when she finally came face-to-face with the twin *bruder* she felt had betrayed his *familye.* Nellie was ready to forgive him for acting like a foolish child and welcome him back into their lives. But would Lydia feel the same way?

"Lydia, would you mind helping me bring in the boxes from the buggy?"

Lydia was happy to get some fresh air. All the dust being stirred up from the workers was making her cough. With the exception of one of the *menner* called *Steve,* Lydia wasn't interested in being around any of them. She'd caught Steve glancing in her direction more than once, and she hoped her *mamm* hadn't noticed. Normally Lydia would never even consider flirting with an *Englischer*, but he had started it, and she wasn't opposed to the idea. Her cousin, Miriam, had dated an *Englischer,* and it had worked out wonderfully for the two of them. Jonathon had taken the baptismal classes and received the baptism, and in the end, Miriam and Jonathon had been married by the Bishop, and are now expecting their first *boppli.*

Lydia shied away from Steve's frequent glances, fearful that he would be able to pick up on her intimate thoughts. If her *mamm* knew she'd been thinking such things, she would be scolded for sure and for certain.

With her own *bruder* as an *Englischer,* Lydia wasn't exactly sure where her thoughts stood on the matter. But the idea of dating an *Englischer* seemed a little more rebellious than she was willing to be for the time-being. Since she hadn't taken the baptism, she wouldn't be shunned for such an action. Lydia wasn't altogether satisfied with her decision not to take the baptism, but it had made sense at the time her *bruder* had left. Truth be told, there were times when she'd second-guessed her lack of commitment to the community, but she wanted to keep her options open as long as was possible. Did her *bruder* know something she didn't? Had being an *Englischer* made him happy? He seemed to be doing alright for himself, but there would be no real way of knowing the truth unless she spoke to him. But the first question that she would have for Liam would be to ask why he hadn't looked back after he'd left.

Chapter 8

Lucy couldn't help but stare out of the bakery window when several *menner* showed up at Nellie's quilting shop next door. They all wore the same blue shirts with the same logo on the pocket that she'd seen the handsome blond stranger wearing. She hadn't seen him loitering across the street yet this morning, and wondered if he would show up. She'd known Liam was interested in construction when he'd left the community, but was it really possible the handsome stranger was him? They'd had a heated discussion about his desire to have his own company just before he'd left. She'd begged him to stay, but he was determined to stand on his own—away from the community.

Lucy looked for the handsome *mann* she thought to be *her* Liam, but he was not with the others when they'd arrived. Part of her wished he would come around again so she could settle the dispute in her mind once and for all, but her heart dreaded the possibility of being broken all over again. Most days, she was able to keep thoughts of Liam out of her mind, but every so often, a memory of him would find its way into her thoughts. Since she'd seen the handsome stranger hanging out across the street from the bakery the past few days, her mind had become consumed with thoughts of Liam again.

A loud crash interrupted her thoughts. How long had she been standing at the window staring out at nothing? The noise had come from the quilt shop next door. With no customers in the bakery, Lucy decided to rush over there to see if everyone was alright.

Liam wiped the paint from his hands before answering his cell phone. It was the third time it had rung, and he knew that meant it was one of his men. He hadn't wanted to answer it because he feared they would ask him to stop by the quilt shop, and he wasn't ready for that just yet.

Holding the phone to his ear with two fingers, Liam anticipated the request from the other end.

"Boss, we need you over here right away. Part of the ceiling collapsed."

Liam's heart lurched forward against his ribcage. "Was anyone hurt?"

Steve coughed. "The owner and her daughter were outside when it happened. I was the only one inside, but I was in the back near the circuit breaker at the time. How soon can you be here?"

Liam looked at the half-painted home he'd been working on most of the day. "If no one was hurt, rope off the area and ask the owner to stay clear until you can be sure there won't be more damage. I'm in the middle of painting, and it would take me at least an hour of cleanup and travel to get there. You can handle this without me. Give my apologies to the owner and explain that I'm in the middle of a job I can't leave right now. I'll be sure to go over with you first thing tomorrow morning."

Steve agreed, but Liam could tell he wasn't buying the excuse he was trying to convince him of. Liam couldn't prevent the ceiling from caving in any more than his employees could. But it was his responsibility to ensure the safety of this crew *and* his family. Guilt consumed him as he continued to paint the small house. He knew he would have to give the paint job to one of the other guys so he could see to the safety of his mother's quilt shop.

Lucy overheard one of the workers calling his boss, which she assumed was Liam. From the worker's end of the conversation, she concluded that the boss had no intention of seeing to the crisis that had unfolded at the quilt shop. Had Liam's exposure to the outside world compromised his integrity? The Liam she had grown to love in her teen years would never have turned his back on his family. But he did, in fact, do that very thing when he became old enough to do so. Was he still so bitter even now that his *familye* still meant nothing to him?

Lucy comforted Nellie, who seemed distraught at the company owner's refusal to see the importance of the immediate danger that the collapsed ceiling posed.

"He doesn't seem like a respectable business owner," Lucy offered.

Nellie held up a hand in defense. "*Nee,* we can't judge a *mann* simply because he isn't able to be here. That Steve fellow said he was stuck at another job and would be here in the morning to check on things. Mr. Yoder recommended we stay out of the building until then, and I think that's wise."

Lucy felt a little unnerved at Nellie's reaction to the recommendation from the company owner they hadn't even met. Was she aware that her son could possibly be the owner? Was Lucy sure of what she'd seen? Perhaps it was best if she herself did not jump to conclusions in order to avoid any possible misunderstanding. Still, she was more than curious to know what his reasons were for not taking this job more seriously, whether he was Liam or not. One thing was certain in Lucy's mind; if the owner of the company Nellie hired was indeed Liam, she now saw him as a bigger coward than she had when they were teenagers.

Nellie and Lydia packed the boxes back into the buggy, intending to leave for the day. Nellie couldn't help but feel discouraged regarding the delay she would endure in opening her shop. More than that, she was disappointed in her only son. Had he become a coward?

Chapter 9

Liam felt confident leaving the paint job in the capable hands of his youngest employee. The young man was the best one who could operate the expensive paint sprayer he'd invested in, so Liam let the job go and followed the others in his white 4x4 to his mother's quilt shop.

Had his men seen how nervous he was before they'd left the office? He had prayed the entire morning, and even breathed a few prayers now while he kept his eye on the road. There was a lot riding on this meeting; it could decide his fate in more ways than one. If all else failed, he would be professional and business-like in order to keep the job for the sake of the men who counted on him so they could pay their bills this month. He would do whatever he could to protect this job from falling through. His personal vested interest in the job and his family would have to be put aside.

When he parked his truck in the alley behind the shops on Main Street, Liam paused and took a deep breath before getting out, asking God for grace. He knew he had a lot of years to make up for to his mother and sister, and it wouldn't be easy even if they allowed him to.

Lord, soften the hearts of my family, and pave the way for me to reunite with them. Bless me with the courage to face them and to endure the heartache if they should choose not to forgive me for abandoning them.

When Liam noticed his crew gathered around his truck, he knew he'd stalled long enough. One more deep breath and Liam swung open his door, easing himself out of his truck. It was now or never, and *never* was just not an option at this point. He tried to swallow the bile that threatened to enter his throat. He would be strong and accept whatever reaction his mother and sister had. He didn't regret being out on his own and starting a business, but he knew he couldn't keep his business and his family too. It had to be one or the other. He had no intention of returning to the community, and that would be the hardest part to make his mother understand.

Liam allowed the others to go ahead of him, while he hung back and examined the damage from the door. His family did not seem to be in the building, so he quickly busied himself checking for major structural damage. His chest tightened when he heard the front door swing open. His back was to the door, and he couldn't bring himself to turn around. Liam felt his mother's eyes bore into the back of his head. He could hear that she hadn't moved from the entryway, as if his presence had flash-frozen her in place.

Lucy stifled every impulse in her to keep from marching over to the quilting shop and demanding to know if the handsome stranger was indeed Liam Yoder. When he stepped out of the white pickup truck, she could see in the blue of his eyes how much he resembled her old beau. When he'd left the Amish community, he'd taken her future hope of marrying and having *kinner* with him.

It's been seven years. Why am I still so chafed about his leaving? I've had plenty of offers since then. Maybe I should have accepted one of them. Except none of them made me happy the way Liam had.

Lucy sighed as she watched her last customer leave the shop. She knew there would be a gap between this one and her lunch rush, but she intended to keep busy, hoping it would take her mind off of what was going on next door. Part of her didn't have the heart to interrupt what she hoped would be a pleasant reunion between Liam and his *familye.* But the part of her that still held onto a little bit of anger for him wanted to storm over there and demand an explanation. Deep down, she knew she didn't have the courage to confront him. Despite her outburst the last time she'd seen Liam, Lucy had been brought up to remain silent rather than voice unpleasant words toward another, but that didn't stop her from feeling the strong desire to do just that.

Nellie stopped in her tracks when she entered her quilt shop. Her own son stood only a few feet from her—the son she hadn't seen in seven years. Her *dochder,* Lydia, who stood next to her, reached out for her hand. Neither of them moved except to cling to one another. Nellie's mouth went dry, preventing her from finding her voice. She watched Liam move further into the depth of the shop as Steve approached them.

"Good to see you again, Mrs. Yoder," Steve said, then tipped his ball-cap toward Lydia. "Miss Yoder."

Lydia's heart beat a little faster as she made eye contact with Steve.

He pointed toward the back of the long shop. "That's my boss, Liam Yoder." Looking between the two, he did a double-take. "I hadn't realized until now that he has the same last name as you do."

Nellie wasn't sure what to say, so she nodded. She figured it was best not to say anything until she'd had the chance to speak to her son away from his employees. It was obvious that he hadn't told them she was his *mamm,* but Liam was a mirror image of his *daed* and looked nothing like her or Lydia. Pain pricked

Nellie's heart at the thought of her own son rejecting her like that. He'd left a lot of hurt in his wake when he'd left home so long ago, but Nellie had tried to fill the void by telling herself it was only temporary. But when weeks turned to months and months turned to years, she'd given up hope of ever setting eyes on him again. Now, here he was, only a few feet from her, and she couldn't muster up the courage to pull Liam into her arms and tell him she'd missed him. Although she had to admit, part of her wanted to take him into the barn and give him a sound lashing for his behavior.

Chapter 10

Liam's heart sped up at the mention of his name. He turned, not looking his mother or sister in the eye. He nodded politely. "Ma'am."

Nellie's throat constricted at the sound of his voice. She noticed immediately that he'd spoken to her using ma'am out of respect rather than using *mamm* as a term of endearment. This was not going to be easy.

Liam began to explain how he intended to put her shop back together to make it good as new, but Nellie didn't hear a word he said. She was too busy biting her bottom lip to keep from sobbing and pulling her son into her arms. He'd grown to be a handsome *mann*—an *Englischer.* If he didn't look so much like his *daed,* she would think he'd managed to fool everyone—everyone but her. Did he think he could come in here and convince her of his act of not knowing her? She could see the fear in his eyes. He knew. He knew that he couldn't hide that from his own *mamm*. Didn't he?

Liam could hear his voice cracking as though he were another person listening to his voice. He wasn't even sure of what he was saying to his mother. All he could think about was how much he'd missed her. But he'd be lucky to keep the job now that she knew it was *his* company that she'd hired to do the renovations to her quilt shop. He hoped she wouldn't fire him and his men. They needed the work, and he intended to do right by his mother for the first time since his dad had died.

He looked into his mother's eyes trying to read her mood. Had she forgiven him for betraying her, or was she being polite the way he was? She seemed pleasant but worried. The lines on her face had deepened since the last time he'd seen her. Her dark brown hair was peppered with gray, and the dark circles surrounding her eyes implied how much sleep she'd probably lost over the past seven years.

Her cordial tone made him nervous. When he was a young boy, the woman could unravel any mischief he'd been up to with only her tone of voice and the look she was giving him now.

I'm a grown man now. I can handle this.

"We expect the renovations to take about three weeks, but as soon as we get the mess cleared away from the ceiling collapse, you should be able to get back in here and work around us. Can you give us until the end of the week to get this mess cleaned up so it's safe for you and your daughter?"

He could see his mother cringe at the formal comment he'd made.

She tipped her mouth into a smile. "Of course, Mr. Yoder, but my *dochder* and I would rather stay and help clean things up."

Liam could see his mother had no intention of budging on the matter. "That's fine as long as you steer clear from the back of the store where the damage is the worst. I can't guarantee your safety back there."

Nellie nodded.

Steve and Jonny flashed Liam a strange look.

"Hey Boss, can we talk to you for a minute outside?"

Liam tipped his hat to his mother and sister before following his employees into the alley.

"What gives?" Jonny complained. "You know we can't have those women in the store when we're trying to clean this mess up. What if they get hurt? We'll all have to give up our pay to take care of their hospital bills."

"I don't think Amish people go to hospitals," Steve said, directing his comment toward Liam.

"Yeah, they are kind of backward, aren't they?" Jonny said with a chuckle.

Even though Liam had said the same thing several times, hearing it from someone else grated on his nerves.

"The daughter is kinda pretty. I'd go out with her," Jonny added.

Liam's breath caught in his throat, causing him to choke. He clenched his fists as he coughed to clear his throat. He wanted to yell at Jonny *That's my sister you're talking about,* but Lydia hadn't been his sister for the past seven years. Still, it was *his* duty to protect her, and he would not let the likes of Jonny lay a hand on Lydia. But as he thought about it, she wouldn't find a better Christian man for her than Steve, who stood politely at his side. The two of them had been friends since high school; Steve had even stood by him during his struggle with his dad's death.

"Let's keep our minds on the current issue," Liam ordered. "The Amish are hard workers, and I'm sure she feels the need to help because it's her shop."

"Since when do you know so much about Amish folks?" Jonny asked.

Liam ignored his flippant remark and turned to address Steve who knew of his past.

"Let the women remain, but everyone is responsible for keeping an eye on them."

Jonny pulled off his ball cap and slapped it against his leg in frustration. "Okay, but if they get hurt, I'm not giving up my pay to send them to the hospital."

Steve waited until Jonny stormed off, and then turned to Liam. “Don’t tell me that’s your family. I’d almost forgotten you were Amish.”

Liam swallowed the lump in his throat. “That is my mother and my sister. I am freaking out a little and don’t know how to deal with them. Seeing them again makes me realize how much I’ve missed them.”

Steve clapped him on the shoulder. “Then tell them that. It’s a good place to start, isn’t it?”

Liam crossed over to his mother’s buggy and petted the familiar horse. “It isn’t that easy, Steve. The Amish are closed off from the rest of the world. I haven’t been shunned, but her strong bond to the church will keep her from reaching out to me.”

Steve managed a half-smile. “I’m sorry, man. Is there anything I can do to make this workable for everyone?”

“For starters, you can keep Jonny away from my sister!”

Steve chuckled. “It would be my pleasure.”

Liam looked at his friend, noting a sudden change in his demeanor.

“Oh my gosh, you like my sister!”

Steve held his hands up playfully. “Don’t kill me, Boss!”

Liam smiled. “I’d be honored to have you as a brother-in-law someday. You’re a good Christian man. But that is up to my sister.”

Steve shook his friend’s hand. “I appreciate that. I feel like she’s been giving me the signal that it’s okay to talk to her. Is that okay with you?”

Liam felt his eyes bulge. “Really? I wouldn’t have ever thought she would consider an *Englischer.* I wonder if she took the baptism. I imagine she felt she had to after I left.”

Steve leaned up against the buggy. “Do you regret leaving?”

“I’m not sure I regret leaving, but I do regret not keeping in touch with my family. I shouldn’t have run off without talking to my mother about it. At the time, I thought I had no other choice. I was just a dumb kid.”

Steve wiped his brow and moved into the shade of the tree that the horse was tethered to. “It’s not too late to change things. You should say this stuff to your mom. There is no shame in admitting you made a mistake. Family is blood and will accept each other no matter what. Your mother seems like a very kind woman. I bet she’d understand. Like you said, you were just a kid.”

Liam remained quiet, processing Steve’s statement. Could it really be that easy? Truth be told, Liam was terrified his mother would turn her back on him. They no longer shared the same faith. But faith was a choice; family was a given.

Chapter 11

Liam realized the only way to figure out if his mother would accept him back into her life would be to wait it out and see how they interacted during the renovation. Only time would tell if reconciliation was possible. For now, there was one more thing he had to do; he had to go next door to the bakery and see if it was indeed *his* Lucy who worked there. If it was her, he could start his apologies with her and see how it went from there. If she received him, chances were good that his family would too.

Standing to the side of the door out of view, Liam took in a few deep breaths preparing himself to enter the bakery. What was he so afraid of? Was it more concern over the possibility of her being married, or was it fear that she would reject him? He knew he still loved her, he always would. But if she'd forgotten him and moved on with her life, he would have a tougher time accepting it and living with the mistake he'd made in leaving her so long ago.

The bells on the door jingled as he opened it slowly. There was no mistaking Lucy's blue eyes and blond hair as she turned to face him. Liam nearly froze in place, mesmerized by the soft, inviting look in her eyes that used to make him weak in the knees. It was odd that she should still have that effect on him. Her eyes cast downward to the box of cookies she was filling for a customer. Liam held back pretending to look at the selection in the glass-front case. He recognized some of Lucy's signature delicacies. He wasn't surprised she was now making a living from her baking skills. He remembered the times she used to surprise him with her newest creation when they were sweethearts. He was always happy to be her taste-tester.

As Liam watched Lucy interact with the *Englisch* customer, he realized she had fulfilled her dream without leaving her family or the Amish ways. Why had he felt that leaving home was the only way to succeed? Had his desire to be like the *Englischers* been more important to him at the time? Being an *Englischer* had not been what he'd expected. He'd thought it meant total freedom, but it hadn't. Being an *Englischer* was not without its own set of problems. Now that he was where he thought he wanted to be in life, all he could think about was going back to the Amish ways.

With the customer's order filled, Lucy looked up into the handsome *Englischer's* face. "May I help you?"

Liam wanted to say so much to her, but all he could manage was to point to the special she had written on the small chalkboard to the side of the counter.

A dozen cookies? What am I going to do with a dozen cookies? Why can't I say what I came in here to say?

Lucy stood at the counter, tongs in hand, staring at Liam. How long had she been staring?

"Would you like all the same or an assortment?"

Liam cleared his throat. "Assortment, please."

Lucy took her time selecting the cookies, allowing him ample time to speak up, but he just couldn't force the words from his brain to his lips. She was more beautiful than he'd remembered her, and all he could do was stare at her. Had she been that beautiful the night he'd left her? His heart fluttered behind his ribcage, and he felt a bead of sweat roll between his shoulder blades and down his spine.

When she finished filling the box, Lucy placed it on top of the glass case, uttering his total. Liam handed her a ten-dollar bill, picked up the cookies and left the store without waiting for his change. More than that, he hadn't said another word to Lucy.

Outside in the warm summer air, Liam tried to catch his breath, but the sun seemed to steal the air from his lungs. How could she have such an effect on him?

He was a grown man. But not grown up enough to apologize, he guessed.

Lucy couldn't believe Liam was walking out of her bakery without so much as a friendly word to her. Had she meant that little to him, that he couldn't even acknowledge her? The very fact he'd left her seven years ago without a second thought gave her the answer she sought. It wasn't what she wanted from him, and she wasn't willing to settle for it. She'd allowed him to leave too easily when they were teenagers, but she was a grown woman now, and capable of speaking her mind. If there was one thing Lucy did not fear, it was confrontation.

Lucy yanked on the tie to her white kitchen apron and slapped it on the counter. She had no customers to deal with, and dealing with Liam's inconsiderate behavior was at the forefront of her agenda. She would wait for the construction workers to leave for lunch, and then she would march over to the quilting shop and confront Liam. He would not get away that easily this time.

Chapter 12

Liam stepped inside the quilt shop, wondering if he would be able to face his own mother after the disaster he'd just encountered with Lucy. He evened his breath and mentally washed Lucy from his thoughts, hoping it would help him concentrate. His heart raced as he approached his mother and sister, who were looking over the supply list with Steve. He paused before interrupting, noting the mutual admiration between his sister and his best friend.

It made him happy that his sister was interested in Steve. In Liam's opinion, there was no one he would rather see Lydia with than his friend. Steve was a good man, and would do right by her. But would their mother allow such a thing? He had no doubt that Steve would convert for Lydia, but with all the negative things he'd said over the years, he wondered how eager Steve would be to succumb to the Amish ways.

Liam's thoughts went back to Lucy. Did he love her enough to go back to being Amish? Did he love his family that much? The answer was a resounding yes, but he feared it was too late.

Steve looked up at him. "Are you going to share that box of goodies, or do you plan on eating them by yourself?"

Liam knew his friend was teasing him, but he suddenly felt uncomfortable. He handed the box of baked goods over to Steve and watched him open it. Did he dare taste the sweet confections made by the hands of the woman he loved? He didn't think he could enjoy her pastries without feeling guilty, especially after the way he'd just handled himself. He'd acted no better than he had when he was a teenager.

Steve clamped his jaw over a sweet treat after offering the women first pick. He held the box out to Liam but he refused. Liam used the excuse that it was too close to lunch time even though he had no appetite at the moment. He was looking forward to the break from having to be polite to his family most of the morning while they worked. His mother had kept her distance, but he'd felt her gaze upon him several times. Liam didn't wonder where he'd inherited his stubbornness from. His mother would let him sweat it out until he came to her. It was her way; had been ever since he could remember.

Nellie asked Steve to show her the plans for renovation, leaving Liam standing alone with Lydia.

She swallowed the last bite of her cookie and leered at her twin brother. "Are you ashamed of us?"

The question startled Liam, who had immediately stuck his nose in the supply list, hoping to buy some time while coming up with something to say to his sister.

"No. Why would you ask such a question?"

Lydia brushed stray blond curls back into her *kapp.* "It seems you want to keep it a secret that you know us—that we are *familye."*

Liam looked into his sister's eyes that burned with anger. "Steve went to school with me. He knows who you are. The rest of my crew doesn't know my past. Not because I'm ashamed of it, but because I don't talk about my personal life."

Lydia poked her brother in the arm. "Why do you think *mamm* opened this shop? She was selling her quilts fine at the flea market. She didn't need to take on a project of this stature. She did it hoping to bring you back into our *familye.* You are bringing shame on her by not acknowledging her."

Liam grabbed a cookie out of the bakery box and bit into it. It was a guilty pleasure he'd tried to deny himself, but now it was more of a distraction than the treat he'd hoped for.

"I suspected she'd opened the shop with me in mind to do the repairs. But I can't change who I am now. Too much time has passed. What do you think the

Bishop will say if he finds out she's keeping company with a member of her family who rejected the baptism to become an *Englischer*? She needs the community and its support, and trying to mend fences with me could weaken that support for her."

Lydia took a deep breath. "She needs you more than she needs the community. We have not been much of a part of the community since—not since *daed's* accident and you left us. I haven't taken the baptism yet."

"You haven't?" Liam was shocked.

"*Nee.* I didn't want to and *mamm* hasn't forced it on me. I think she's afraid that if she does I will leave her like you did."

Liam ran his fingers through his dark blond hair. "I'm sorry for leaving the way I did, but at the time I was an emotional kid and didn't think it through. By the time I realized it was a mistake, it was too late to turn back."

Lydia placed her hand on his. "It's never too late to come home. We miss you."

Liam pulled his sister into a hug, and fought the tears that formed behind his eyes. "I've missed you both so much. But I had a tough time dealing with the accident. It was my fault he died. I should have been there to save him."

Lydia pulled away from her twin. "It was not your fault. If you'd been there, *mamm* would more than likely be mourning your death too."

"Hasn't she already mourned the loss of her son all this time?" Liam couldn't hold in the tears any longer. He lowered his head to disguise his pain.

"I suppose she has," Lydia said quietly.

"I've really made a mess of this haven't I?"

Lydia sniffled. "It doesn't have to be a mess. You can fix it."

"I don't think I know how."

Lydia looked him firmly in the eye. "You can start by taking responsibility for the wrong you've done. We are ready to forgive and forget, but first you have to be repentant of the sins you committed against your *familye.*"

Liam knew it was the right thing to do, but he didn't know how to give up being an *Englischer*.

Chapter 13

Lucy pulled on the front door to the quilt shop, spotting Liam toward the back of the long room. She slammed the door, watching bits of plaster filter down from the holes in the ceiling. She chided herself, knowing how hard Nellie had worked at cleaning the floor near the front of the shop. She'd have to make it up to her later. For now, her target was Liam, who'd stopped in his tracks when she slammed the front door. Now, he watched her approach, fear in his eyes the way an animal looks just before the conclusion of the hunt. She almost enjoyed the fear she saw in his eyes as she approached him, fists on her hips. When she closed the space between them, he flinched.

"Are you going to slap me again?" he asked, holding his arms in front of him defensively.

The grim line of Lucy's mouth broke when her lips parted to speak. "I should! How dare you come into my bakery after all these years and not say a word to me."

Liam backed up a step. "I had intended to say a lot of things, but I couldn't force myself to say them. I figured you've moved on with your life and probably have a family of your own and wouldn't care what I had to say anyway."

Lucy looked into his blue eyes that used to delight her when she gazed upon them. Now all she saw was a handsome stranger in front of her. She longed for him to pull her into his arms and whisper that everything was going to be alright, but it wasn't, and she couldn't allow herself to hope for such a childish whim.

"Just because I've moved on with my life doesn't mean I don't want to know where you've been all these years."

She wouldn't tell him she didn't have a husband or *kinner;* she wouldn't let him off the hook that easily. Besides, she didn't want him knowing the truth. She'd held out hope for his return all these years and had wasted that time wishing for something that would never come to pass.

"There isn't much to tell," he admitted with the pain of realization that the last seven years had been devoid of what he'd had with her. He'd taken her for granted, and he'd had to live with that regret all this time.

"There isn't much to tell?" she asked through gritted teeth. "You're an *Englischer.* Look at you. I barely recognize you anymore."

Liam heard creaking above him as he mindlessly watched bits of plaster dust float to the floor like dry, powdery snow.

"You knew when I left the community I intended to explore the *Englisch* ways. I may look like an *Englischer* on the outside, but in my heart, I will always be Amish."

It was the first time he'd really thought about it, but he'd meant every word of it. He didn't feel *Englisch* at all, despite his physical appearance. His heart would always be with his family—with Lucy. So why had it taken him this long to realize it? He wanted to pull her into his arms and tell her he still loved her, but it was obvious she had a family of her own now.

Lucy took a step toward him. "You can't have a foot in both worlds. You made a choice when you left the community, and now you will have to live with that choice."

Liam scoffed at her. "I don't have a foot in both worlds. And that decision doesn't have to be set in stone."

Lucy narrowed her eyes. "You're right. You are fully *Englisch.* You made the choice."

Liam was very aware of her every move. Her skirts wavered from the slight breeze blowing in the building from the open back door. The air around her seemed almost animated as it swirled up the plaster dust that fell from the ceiling. How could he make her understand why he'd stayed away for so long when he didn't even understand it himself? It was too late. He'd destroyed his relationship with his family *and* with her.

Liam lifted his hands in surrender. "You're right. I can't live in both worlds, but I don't know how to go back. Too much time has passed already. Our lives have changed. We're grown up and have separate lives no matter where I stand."

Lucy studied him for a moment. Was he talking about the two of them *or* his family?

"You can go home any time you want, but you can't have it both ways."

Liam turned his back on Lucy. "I've disappointed everyone I care about. I can't do the same thing to these men that depend on me for a job. It's too late for me to go home. This is my life now whether I like it or not."

Lucy spoke softly around the lump forming in her throat. "I imagine your *mamm* would see it differently than you do."

Liam whipped around to face her. "What about you, Lucy? How do you see things?"

A single tear rolled down her cheek and she flicked it angrily. "It no longer matters what I think. Too much time has passed for us. But time stood still for your *mamm.* She's been waiting for you all this time. It's *her* time. She deserves to have her son return to her."

Lucy gazed upon his handsome face. She couldn't admit it to him that she herself had waited all these years hoping and praying for his return. The sense of betrayal would not allow her to admit she would always love him. Looking at him now was like looking into her past. He was her past and he needed to remain there for the sake of her heart. If she allowed him into her fragile heart again, it would surely break beyond repair.

Liam reached out to her, but she backed away.

"I'm sorry," he managed softly.

"Please don't come into the bakery anymore. It's best if we don't see each other anymore."

The ceiling creaked while fresh clumps of plaster fell all around Liam. Lucy turned and walked toward the open back door. Before she reached the entrance that led out to the alley, she turned to look at Liam once more, determined it would be the last time she laid eyes on him. The truth was it hurt too much to see him, and she needed to get over him once and for all.

Chapter 14

Lucy stood in the doorway of the quilt shop watching helplessly as a large portion of the ceiling collapsed onto Liam. Her feet remained planted in place as though frozen for what seemed like several minutes, when in reality only a few seconds had passed. Rushing to his side, she coughed from the cloud of plaster dust that had camouflaged the severity of the damage.

Tears clutched Lucy's throat as she tugged at a large board that had connected with Liam's head, but she couldn't budge the large section of ceiling under which he was trapped, that she estimated to be about ten feet wide. He groaned from the pain, and Lucy was grateful to hear he still had some life in him, though he lay motionless on the floor in the pile of rubble. She prayed frantically in her mind while brushing white plaster from Liam's face.

"Liam, please wake up! Open your eyes—please! I didn't mean the things I said to you…I still love you." She pleaded with him, but he barely stirred.

Muffled ringing interrupted her immediate thoughts. It was coming from the cell phone in his shirt pocket. She lifted the phone to her ear after pressing the *talk* button.

"Help," she said weakly to the person on the other end of the line. "Liam's been hurt. The ceiling of his mother's quilt shop collapsed and I'm afraid he's dying."

"This is Steve, who am I talking to?"

Lucy remembered Steve as being one of Liam's employees.

"This is Lucy Graber, I own the bakery next to the quilt shop. Can you help me? I can't move the piece of plaster board off him. It's too large."

"I'll send an ambulance, and I'll be there in just a few minutes myself."

Lucy dropped Liam's phone on the dirty floor and picked his head up, placing it gently on her lap. She smoothed his dark blond hair and pressed the corner of her apron to the cut in his hairline that the plank of wood had created. She lightly blew the plaster dust from his eyelashes, causing them to flutter.

His lashes fluttered a few more times and his breathing seemed shallow. Lucy whispered a prayer as she continued to stroke his hair lovingly. She'd dreamed of holding him again, and now that she had him close to her, she wished the circumstances could be different. She feared she would never get the chance to tell him she still loved him. Why had she wasted time arguing with him instead of declaring her love for him?

Then another thought occurred to her. Had Lydia and Nellie gone home for the day? She'd already exposed his past to his employee when he called a few minutes before. Liam would surely never forgive her for such an act of betrayal. But how could she blame him when she hadn't forgiven him for leaving her seven long years ago.

Lucy leaned down and placed a kiss on Liam's cheek. "I forgive you," she whispered. "I've not stopped loving you. I will follow you into the *Englisch* world if that's what it takes to never lose you again. I'm sorry I didn't follow you when you asked me to when we were eighteen."

Lucy began to sob. "I could have been your *fraa*. We would have had a *wunderbaar* wedding with our *familye* and friends. We could have had at least four *kinner* by now. They would all be as beautiful as you. Our girls would have bouncing blond curls and they would sit at your feet as you read the scripture. Our boys would be strong and work hard in the barn with you mucking the stalls and milking the cows. Our *dochdern* would help me plant in the kitchen garden while you and the boys were plowing the fields for planting season. We would have *wunderbaar* meals together and I would make your favorite deserts for after. I remember how much you like my baking."

Liam stirred a little, his facial expression displaying grief. Lucy imagined he was in a lot of pain, and with the weight of the large section of plaster board that still lay across his torso, she worried his breathing would stop altogether.

Lucy hiccupped a staggered breath from crying so hard. "I promise my sweet Liam that I will spend the rest of my days with you if you hang on long enough. Your *mamm* and Lydia aren't even here. Please don't die before you can reunite with them—with me."

Liam's eyes fluttered open and closed a few times, and Lucy prayed he could see her. "Shhh," she soothed him. "Everything is going to be alright. Help is on the way."

She leaned down and kissed him again, allowing her lips to linger thoughtfully on his cheek.

"I'm so sorry for slapping you all those years ago. I wanted to hold onto you and never let you go, but you were determined to leave me. I felt helpless. I don't think I stopped crying for at least three months after you left. I kept hoping you would get a taste of the outside world and come back begging me to reconcile. But you never did. After a while, I hardened my heart and refused to let anyone in my heart. I was asked to court many times, but you were always the only one I ever wanted. You are my true love."

Liam's eyes fluttered open and remained there about a half slit. "Lucy," he managed so low, she barely heard him.

Lucy cradled his head closer to her and kissed his forehead. "I'm here, Liam. I love you. I've never stopped loving you."

Out of the corner of her eye, Lucy could see Steve standing in the doorway that led to the alley. Panic traveled through her like a lightning strike as she wondered how long he'd been standing there and how much of her one-sided conversation he'd overheard.

Chapter 15

Steve rushed into the room and knelt down beside his boss and friend. He turned to Lucy and looked at her thoughtfully. "If you help me, I think we can move this piece of plaster board without hurting him. I'm going to lift and try to shove it clear of him. I need you to try to keep him still. When I move this, he may shift and it could cause more damage."

Lucy nodded as she held tight to his free arm and cradled his head in her lap.

With one swift movement, Steve picked up on the edge of the large section of ceiling and pushed until it was clear of Liam's body. Liam groaned and tried to move, but Lucy steadied him with her free hand.

Steve knelt down and checked Liam's pulse.

"His pulse is strong so that's a good sign. But we probably should try not to move him in case anything is broken. How did he get the gash in his forehead?"

Lucy pointed to the long board she'd moved after the accident. "That hit him in the head. It was still across his head, but I moved it."

"Is he still bleeding?"

Lucy eased the pressure on his head wound noting that the blood had stopped. She smoothed out her apron not caring that it was stained with blood. In the distance, she could hear the siren from the ambulance drawing near the shop. Relief washed over her when they pulled into the alley and stopped where Lucy could see them.

Two men jumped out of the ambulance and opened the back to retrieve a stretcher. They wheeled it in next to Liam and set a big box of medical supplies next to him. Lucy tried to wriggle out from under him, but the paramedics told her to stay put to keep him stable until they could check his vitals.

"Has he regained consciousness at all?" one of them asked Lucy.

"He hasn't woken up, but he's groaned a few times. He opened his eyes a few times, and I thought he looked right at me. He said my name, but he's been out for the most part."

"That's a good sign that he recognized you. Do you know him?" the paramedic asked as he looked into Liam's eyes with a small, pen-sized flashlight.

Lucy hesitated as she gazed upon Steve, but then she nodded. "*Jah,* we are old friends."

"Will you be riding with him to the hospital, Miss?" the paramedic asked.

"Someone has to tell his *familye* what happened. They don't have a phone."

Steve stepped forward. "Write down the address and I'll bring them to the hospital. You go with Liam. He needs you."

Lucy could see the sincerity in Steve's face, and it eased her worries just a little.

"I have to lock up the bakery next door. I'll be right back."

The paramedics nodded as they lifted Liam onto the stretcher. He groaned and coughed, curling and clutching at his right side. Lucy ran next door and closed the bakery and hurried out the back door into the alley, locking it behind her.

As she approached the ambulance, they were sliding the stretcher into the back. One paramedic slid into place beside the stretcher, while the other assisted Lucy into the back. He closed the doors behind her and went up front to drive to the hospital.

When they pulled into Elkhart General Hospital, Lucy realized she hadn't asked Steve to let her own *familye* know she wouldn't be home. She hoped that when her *bruder* came back to the bakery at the end of the day to pick her up that he would think she'd gotten a ride from Nellie and Lydia. She hadn't thought to leave a note on the door for him, and hoped he wouldn't worry until word could be sent home.

After the ambulance came to a stop at the emergency entrance, the driver opened the back door and assisted Lucy out first. The paramedics wheeled Liam inside where they listed off his condition to a waiting nurse who wheeled him out of Lucy's sight.

Taking a seat in a nearby chair in the waiting room feeling unsure of what she should do, Lucy kept an eye on the set of double-doors behind which Liam disappeared. Within minutes a nurse approached her with a clipboard and asked if she could fill out the papers for Liam.

Grateful for something to do, she listed his name and birthdate along with other information she knew about him. She had thought she knew everything there was to know about him, but the fact remained that he'd been a stranger to her for the past seven years. She could easily list his history, but she had no idea what to say for anything current.

Frustrated, she put the unfinished papers in the chair next to her, staring once again at the double-doors hoping someone would invite her back to sit with Liam.

Nearly dozing off in the chair from boredom, Lucy was startled when a nurse approached her.

"Are you with the young man that was brought in by the ambulance?"

"*Jah.* Is he awake?"

"He's been mumbling the name *Lucy.* Is that you?"

Lucy nodded with downcast eyes and then followed the nurse after she took the clipboard with Liam's information on it.

"I'm sorry I couldn't fill out everything. There are a few things I don't know."

The nursed waived her off. "Don't worry about it. As long as we have his name, we can get the rest later when he wakes up."

"Is he going to be alright?" Lucy was almost afraid of the answer.

"We'll know more when we get the results of his x-rays. But for now, he's stable."

Lucy wasn't sure if that was good news or not, but as long as he was still breathing, she would be thankful.

Chapter 16

Lucy stood in the doorway of the room where they had Liam. His chest was exposed and he had wires connected to little round discs. She had seen the same things on her mother when she'd been in the hospital having surgery on her gallbladder. She also knew that the tubing in Liam's nose was feeding him oxygen.

"Don't be afraid to talk to him," the nurse urged her. "It might help to wake him up if he hears a familiar voice.

The nurse pulled a chair over to Liam's bedside and invited her to sit. She wasn't sure how much good her voice would do to help stir Liam from his slumber, but she was willing to give it a try. It seemed to keep him slightly alert while at the quilt shop just after the ceiling collapsed onto him.

Lucy sat down in the chair, unsure of what to do. She was grateful when the nurse excused herself after telling her that she would be right outside at the desk if Liam should need anything. She reassured Lucy that they were monitoring Liam from there, which made her feel a little more at ease.

Lucy stared at Liam; his torso exposed to the waist. His chest was quite sculpted compared to the way he looked when she knew him as a teenager. His arms were taught with muscles and his skin was smooth except for the occasional scratch in his skin. Bruises had risen to the surface of his skin around his ribcage, and she suspected he'd suffered a few broken ribs. She recalled her brother having the same discoloration when he'd broken three ribs after a fall from the loft in the barn when they were kids.

Lucy slipped her hand into Liam's warm hand. It still fit nicely, sending a spark of exhilaration down her spine. The cut in his hairline had strips of tape over it, but no one had cleaned the bloodstains from his cheek. She rose from the chair, reluctantly letting Liam's hand drop, and went over to the sink and pulled paper towels from the dispenser. She wet them and stepped over to Liam, wiping his face clean.

"Now this is something I imagined doing as your *fraa.* Not that I've imagined having to mop up blood from your face. But I always thought I would take care of you when you were ill. It's what I'd wanted to do since the first day I laid eyes on you."

Liam didn't stir, so she went on.

"I can't believe I've loved you since I was fifteen years old. Ten years is a long time to love a *mann* when you're not his *fraa*."

That statement seemed to get a reaction out of him. He stirred but didn't open his eyes.

"Lucy," he managed with a weak voice.

She tossed the wet towels in the trash and stood at his bedside. "I'm here. Can you open your eyes?"

She lowered herself to the edge of the bed despite the inner voice telling her she shouldn't be so brazen. But she just couldn't help herself. She was so drawn to him and longed to be near him that she didn't care what it looked like. She still loved him, and they had lost a lot of time. If something happened to him and he didn't survive this accident, she'd never be able to live with herself if she didn't at least try to win him back.

Lucy pulled his hand into hers. She admired the lines of his muscles that defined his chest as she watched him breathe. It was comforting to her that his hand was warm, because to her, that meant he was still with her. She couldn't leave his side. She feared that if she blinked he would leave her.

Liam's face seemed serene, as though he was deep in a good dream. She hoped it was so. She hated the thought of him being in pain.

Why hadn't she gone after him all those years ago? He'd offered to marry her and take her with him, but she'd turned him down without a second thought. If she had it to do all over again, she surely would say yes if given another chance.

Gott, please give me another chance with Liam. I love him. I've never stopped loving him, but you already know that. Please don't let me lose him all over again. Breathe life into his body.

Her prayer seemed selfish, she knew, but it was all she could think about. She needed him to recover so she could tell him she still loved him. Now that she was faced with the possibility of losing him again, she couldn't bear it.

Lucy felt Liam's hand close gently over hers. Her heart quickened its pace at the thought of him reaching out to her and connecting with her.

"Liam, can you hear me? It's me, Lucy. I'm here for you. Please wake up."

"Lucy." He coughed and then groaned from the pain. "I thought you were mad at me."

Lucy stared at Liam, who hadn't opened his eyes. Was he dreaming, or was he talking to her? Either way, talking *had* to be a *gut* sign—wasn't it?

"I'm not mad at you anymore. I forgave you a long time ago."

Liam tried to move, but winced from the pain, his eyelids fluttering. "But—our fight last night. You slapped me."

Lucy was confused. Had the bump on his head caused him to be disoriented? They had just fought about two hours ago, and though she'd threatened to slap him, she hadn't.

"Liam, I didn't slap you. I'm sorry for yelling at you, though."

Liam reached a hand to his eyes and rubbed them. "*Jah,* you slapped me when I told you I was leaving you to start a new life as an *Englischer.*"

Chapter 17

Lucy's heart skipped a beat. Was he delirious from the accident, or did Liam really think that their argument they'd had seven years ago had happened just last night?

"Liam, please open your eyes," Lucy said impatiently.

His eyelids fluttered. "Everything is blurry. Where am I?"

Liam squinted against the bright fluorescent lights of the emergency room.

"You're at the hospital. Do you remember what happened?"

Lucy didn't want to say too much before she gave him a chance to wrap his mind around being in the hospital. He *had* to know he was hurt, didn't he?

Liam tried to sit up, but quickly laid back down, groaning and clutching his bruised ribs.

"Where's *mei mamm* and *daed?"*

Lucy's heart caught in her throat when she heard him ask for *both* his parents. Had he blocked out the last seven years? How could she break the news to him that his *daed* had died so long ago? Perhaps it was best to avoid the question for now and give Liam a chance to wake fully. Not only was he not making any sense, but he was talking the way he used to when they were young. He'd spoken like an *Englischer* when they'd argued earlier.

"Steve went to your *haus* to get your *familye."*

Liam placed a hand over his eyes to shield the bright lighting in the room. "How do you know Steve?"

Lucy knew she needed to tread lightly on her answers until he remembered where he was in terms of time. She guessed he had a concussion, and his full memory would return as soon as he gained his bearings.

"Steve is your friend from school. He was there when the boards fell on you. Don't you remember anything about your accident?"

"My head is pounding and it hurts to open my eyes. I'm surprised you're still speaking to me after our fight."

Lucy was confused. If he thought their fight was the previous night, why didn't he remember his *daed* was gone? His *daed* had died a month before their big fight. Lucy decided to play along to see just how much he remembered—at least until the nurse returned.

"I changed my mind. I decided I would very much like to be a part of your life as an *Englischer.*"

Liam lifted her hand to his and kissed it. "I'm so happy to hear that. I want so much to have my own business one day and build houses. You'll see; we will have a *gut* life together."

Lucy knew she had to be careful or she would buy into the dream that Liam had so colorfully laid out for the two of them. In reality she felt it was too late for them. But she did still love him, and wondered if that would be enough. Would he be angry with her when he regained his bearings and remembered where they were in their lives, or would he be happy for another chance to start over with her?

"What about your *familye?*"

"*Mei dead* already knows I'm going to school. He promised he would be at my graduation next month. *Mei mamm* will come around to the idea. He told me he was going to talk to her about coming with him."

Why didn't he remember about his *daed's* accident? It seemed odd that he should remember their argument, but thought that it had taken place a month earlier than it had. Lucy guessed that explained why he still thought his *daed* was still alive. She decided she should test him.

"Liam do you know what month it is?"

He tried to open his eyes again, but winced with pain. "I know I hit my head; I can feel it. But I know it's May because I'm graduating next month. I'll be eighteen the day after I graduate and we can be married then."

He thinks he's still seventeen years old! What is he going to think if he sees me? I've aged in the last seven years! What if he doesn't like what he sees? What if he thinks I'm too old? Gott, I know this isn't kind, but please keep Liam's vision blurry until his memory is intact.

Lucy knew it wasn't right to pray for such a selfish thing, but she feared losing him again. But when his memory came back, would he remember that he no longer loved her? The situation seemed almost hopeless, but Lucy was determined to hold onto whatever tiny shred of hope she could cling to.

Liam squeezed her hand. "You're being very quiet. Am I worse off than you're telling me?"

Lucy giggled nervously. "Everything is going to be fine, Liam. You just need some rest."

"I hope you're right because I can't miss the last few weeks of school or I won't graduate. *Daed* is so proud of me. I don't want to let him down."

Lucy never realized just how supportive Liam's *daed* had been as a willing party to his attendance at the public school. She'd assumed all these years that Liam had been rebellious, and that was why he'd left the community. Was it possible that he'd had his father's blessing in all of it? Why then, did he seem so rebellious after his *daed* died? Why had he left so late at night after leaving his *mamm* a note? Perhaps he was hurting more than Lucy had given him credit for at the time. Was it possible that was the reason he was now blocking out the accident that took his father's life?

Liam tried to shift on the narrow emergency room bed. He groaned from the pain. "You're being quiet again. You haven't changed your mind about marrying me have you?"

Lucy cupped his cheek lovingly. "Of course not. I love you. I've always loved you."

It wasn't a lie even though it felt like one. She hadn't stopped loving him, but she feared he'd stopped loving her a long time ago.

Chapter 18

Lucy sat in the waiting room while more tests were being run on Liam. She was also waiting for Nellie and Lydia so she could fill them in on what was happening with Liam. The nurse had advised her that the loss of memory and blurry vision was usually temporary, but she feared she would have to continue the charade indefinitely if he didn't heal. But would that really be so bad? It might seem a little like taking advantage of a sick *mann,* but it might also be a way to get back together with Liam, and Lucy was pretty sure that was what she wanted. After all, it was what she'd been dreaming of for the past seven years. So why was she suddenly apprehensive?

If only there was a way to know if his sudden declaration of love for me was coming from his heart now, or only from his memories of the past.

Gott, please heal Liam's body and mind. Help him to remember me and his familye. Spare him the pain of learning all over again that his daed is no longer with us. Give his mamm and Lydia the strength to forgive him for the past and help him put his life back together now. I need strength too, so that I am able to let go of the past. If it is your will, please reconcile Liam with his familye—and with me.

Lucy looked at the clock on the wall of the waiting room. She was certain that her *familye* would be getting ready for the evening meal. Within an hour, she would be expected at home. She wanted to stay at the hospital, but wasn't sure if her *daed* would still be in the barn to hear the phone if she called to let him know where she was. Deciding it was worth a try, Lucy went to the nurse's desk to ask if she would allow her to make a call.

Luckily, her *daed* answered on the third ring. His stern voice practically insisted she come home, but when Lucy firmly refused his offer to send her *bruder* to pick her up, understanding changed his tone. Lucy was a grown woman, capable of making her own decisions, but she knew her *daed* still wanted to hold onto his *dochder* a little longer.

Lucy returned to her seat in the waiting room feeling discouragement settle in her heart. Her thoughts were muddled with conflicting thoughts, and none of it made any sense to her. A few hours ago she had told Liam she never wanted to see him again, but just minutes ago she was declaring her love for him all over again. Was Liam the only one that was confused? The difference was that she hadn't hit her head. She had no excuse for her behavior. It was all a lie—or was it?

The truth was a scary thing for her to admit, but she knew in her heart she could never love another *mann* as long as she drew breath into her lungs. Liam was the one her very soul yearned for. If she was capable of loving another, she'd have her own *familye* by now, but she could never bring herself to accepting the affections of any other suitor—and there had been plenty who'd called on her after Liam left. She had never been able to look beyond the love she held so dear in her heart for the one *mann* who'd betrayed her. She suddenly wondered if he'd remained as faithful to her all these years as she had been to him. Was it possible that Liam had experienced the love of another woman while living as an *Englischer*?

The very thought of it boiled her blood. It roiled in her stomach like fire. She'd made a fool of herself declaring love for a *mann* she hadn't seen for seven long years. He was as *Englischer,* capable of betraying her in the worst way. Sudden panic seized her thoughts, sending her fleeing to the restroom.

Locking the door behind her, she studied her reflection in the mirror. Small crinkles stretched from the corners of her eyes, her cheeks and nose peppered with light freckles. There was no doubt that she had aged since the last time Liam had seen her. Was it any wonder he didn't speak to her when he'd entered her bakery earlier? She'd seen how beautiful the *Englisch* women looked with their makeup to hide the flaws, and eye powders that brought out the color in their eyes better. She looked plain and simple compared to the women that frequented her bakery. Why would Liam choose to stay true to her when he was handsome enough to get the attention of any of those women who were much more beautiful than she was?

Tears welled up in her eyes, bringing anger to her heart. So far she had refused the baptism, and it had caused a rift between her and her parents. They knew that the reasons for her rejection of the baptism and of the suitors who'd made their intentions known to her was because of her love for Liam. They hadn't pushed her, for fear she would run off to find Liam. But she knew she couldn't put it off much longer. She was nearly twenty-five years old, and it was only a matter of time before she would be expected to make the commitment or leave home. Unfortunately, she wasn't prepared to do either at this time.

Turning on the faucet, Lucy dipped her hands in the cool water and splashed it on her heated cheeks. The next handful washed over her swollen eyes. A few more splashes and she would feel better—she hoped.

Looking at her reflection again, she pulled several paper towels from the holder on the wall next to her. As she wiped her face, she wondered if she could overlook such an offense. If Liam had betrayed her with another woman sometime in the past seven years, could she take him back? Was he capable of such an act of betrayal? He certainly hadn't made any attempt to contact her. Perhaps he was perfectly happy in the *Englisch* world.

Chapter 19

Lucy finally left the restroom feeling more discouraged than when she'd gone in. Why had she refused her *daed's* prompting to send her *bruder* to bring her home? Now she was stuck at the hospital, and would have to wrestle with her conflicting feelings in front of Nellie and Lydia. How could she go back into Liam's room when he thought they were still in love? How could she continue to pretend that the last seven years apart had not occurred? If he had found love with another woman in that amount of time, he didn't show it, but that didn't mean it hadn't happened.

Gott, please show me what to do. I don't want to hurt Liam, but I don't want to get hurt either. Please spare our hearts from being broken further from this mess. I love him, Gott, I do. But I don't know if I could forgive him if he's betrayed me with the love of another woman. Please bring this to light before my heart is invested too deeply in Liam again.

Outside of Liam's room, Lucy heard a doctor trying to coax him into remembering the correct date.

She felt bad for him as he struggled. Thankfully, the doctor didn't confuse him further by revealing Liam's mistake. Deciding it was best to leave Liam in the capable hands of the doctor, Lucy went back to the waiting room to wait for Nellie and Lydia. What could possibly be taking them so long to arrive? Perhaps Steve had a little trouble finding their farm.

Before she had too much time to think about it, the two women walked into the emergency room with Steve close behind them.

Nellie rushed to her side. "How is my *buwe?"*

Lucy's throat constricted at the distress on Nellie's face. "He's awake, but he's disoriented."

Relief washed over Nellie's face, and Lucy hated to give her worse news, but she figured it was better coming from her than from a stranger.

"Liam's vision is a little blurry and he is having trouble with his memory. The doctor said it was usually temporary, but he has lost the last seven years. Liam thinks he's still only seventeen—and he was asking for his *daed."*

Nellie covered her mouth to stifle the sobs that tried to escape. Lucy placed a comforting hand on her shoulder, but the woman drew strength back into her expression and raised her chin defiantly.

"Perhaps this is *Gott's* way of giving us a second chance with him."

Nellie was right.

This Liam loved her, and when he regained his memory, there was a *gut* possibility that he would retain that love in his heart for her. It was the second chance she'd asked for, and it was up to her to put the past behind them and leave it there.

Lydia stepped forward. "Where is he? I need to see *mei bruder*. The last two conversations I've had with him were not full of kind words, and I'd like to remedy that."

Guilt had filled Lydia during the ride over to the hospital to the point she couldn't even enjoy being pressed up against Steve in the cab of his truck. She'd wanted to savor the moment of closeness with Steve, but all she could think about were the harsh words she'd spoken to Liam.

Nellie walked over to an empty corner of the waiting room. "I need to sit for a moment before I go in and see him. You go ahead and visit with him, Lydia. I'll be along after I gather my thoughts."

Lydia and Steve followed Lucy through the double doors to where Liam rested.

Nellie sat down with a thud. She felt as though the wind had been stricken from her lungs. Memories of her husband's accident rushed through her mind as she steadied herself on the waiting room chair. What had been seven long years ago seemed suddenly like it was only yesterday that she had sat in this very room while she waited to hear the news that her husband had not survived the accident. She hadn't even had the chance to tell him goodbye.

Now as she contemplated the outcome of her son's accident, she felt paralyzed with fear. How could she go in there and tell her son all over again that his *daed* was no longer with them? How could she break his heart like that a second time? The last time she'd told him he ran from her. Would he do the same thing all over again? They'd just found each other after being apart too long, and Nellie wasn't willing to lose her son again so soon.

Gott, bless me with the words to tell my son that his daed is with you. Spare his heart from breaking, and give him the strength to endure this news a second time. Preserve my familye, and help us to use this trial to bring us closer together. Preserve Liam's memories and return them to him so that he can be strong in your word. If this is your way of blessing us with a second chance to reconcile our familye, then guide us to use this opportunity wisely.

Nellie rose from the chair determined to take care of her son no matter what the outcome.

Chapter 20

Nellie stiffened her jaw and swallowed down her fear as she neared her son's hospital room. She told herself as she set her gaze upon him that the important thing was that he was still with her. She had to hold onto that in order to get her through. She'd spoken to the doctor and knew what she was up against. She would do as he instructed and keep the news of his *daed* from him for the time-being. The doctor had stated that added stress could cause him to revert further into his past memories. She certainly didn't want to be the cause of her son having a mental breakdown.

It wouldn't be easy to keep the truth from Liam, but she had taken the time to put together a reasonable excuse for why her husband was not with her. She only hoped her son would accept it.

Nellie stood in the doorway of Liam's room and took a deep breath, pasting a smile on her face. It didn't matter that her son probably couldn't see her smiling, but it helped to ease the pain in her aching heart. She was almost grateful that her son's vision would be blurry for a while, as she worried he would be shocked at how much she had aged over the past seven years.

Stepping quietly into the room, she moved slowly toward Liam's bedside. His ribs were bruised and his head was red and swollen near his hairline. The steady whirring sound from the oxygen that streamed into his nose through narrow tubing filled the room. Nellie hated awkward silence, and was grateful for the little bit of noise the oxygen provided. The room smelled strongly of disinfectant, and Nellie fought to keep her stomach from retching. A monitor to the side of the bed beeped repetitiously with every beat of her son's heart, and the sound was comforting to Nellie. It meant that her son was breathing and his heart was strong. Something she'd always taken for granted—until now.

Nellie lowered herself carefully into the chair beside the bed, trying not to intrude on her son's slumber. She was content with watching him breathe, even though she was eager to see him awake. Her maternal instincts urged her to lift the covers over Liam to protect him from the chill in the room, but she opted not to disturb him.

Though he'd cut his thick blond hair short to mimic the styles of the *Englisch,* Nellie could still see the strong resemblance to his *daed* when she looked at Liam. She'd fallen in *lieb* with Liam's *daed* because of the same rebellious streak she noted their son had inherited. How could she fault him for growing up to be so much like his *daed?* If not for his love for Nellie and his eagerness to marry her, her husband wouldn't have taken the baptism either. Now she was left with his two *kinner* who had taken their *daed's* rebellion a little too literally. Perhaps it was time she left the community and clung to her children. They were all she had left from her husband, and she didn't want to lose them too. Surely *Gott* would forgive her as long as she held fast to her faith.

Nellie let her thoughts drift to the day Liam and Lydia were born. The pregnancy had been almost unbearable, and would have done her in if not for her husband doting on her the way he had. She remembered the proud look on her husband's face when Liam was born first. She hadn't been aware she was carrying twins, and had felt a little disappointment until she saw the admiration in his *daed's* eyes. Then when the pains intensified once more, she feared something was wrong until the midwife had presented her with her *dochder*.

Then after, when they'd rushed her to the hospital after her uterine wall had ruptured, she nearly lost her life. Her husband was by her side the entire time, while her *schweschder* filled in as wet-nurse for her twins. She recalled how supportive her husband had been when he learned she could have no further *kinner*.

Their *familye* had survived many trials over the years, but the death of her husband had unraveled them. Now that is was up to her, she would weave her *familye* back together no matter how much work it presented. She would make certain her son knew how much she loved him, and how much he was wanted back home where he belonged.

Liam stirred, bringing Nellie out of her reverie.

"*Mamm?*"

It was a simple word, but it meant the world to her to hear that from his lips. It wasn't the polite Ma'am that it had been only yesterday. Now it was the term of endearment she hadn't heard from him for seven long years.

Nellie stood up, placing her hand protectively over her son's.

"I'm here."

A slight smile tipped the corners of his mouth.

"Where's Lydia and *Daed?*"

Nellie's lips narrowed as she swallowed hard. This was it. She was about to lie to her son. Before she could muster up the courage to speak the words, Liam drifted back to sleep. She breathed a heartfelt prayer of thanks that she didn't have to say the words just yet. She knew it was only a matter of time before he woke fully and asked the question again. For now, she was in the clear.

Nellie slumped back down into the chair beside the bed, willing her heart to slow enough to catch her breath. Anxiety gripped her in a way it hadn't since the death of her husband. She wasn't ready to relive the painful memories she'd worked so hard to bury along with the *mann* she loved. If he were here with her now, he would provide her with the support she needed. For the first time since his death, she would have to rely on her own strength to get her through. It was times like this one that keeping her hands busy helped to quiet her mind. After her husband died, quilting had been the only thing to keep her idle hands from wringing with anxiety. Now, as she sat at her son's bedside, she wished for a needle and quilt squares to keep her mind and hands too busy to let worry set in.

Chapter 21

Lydia squeezed into the middle of Steve's truck once again, while Lucy sat in the passenger's side. *Mamm* had told them to go home since Liam had been transferred to a private room and had not woken up even once. He didn't even stir when the nurses had wrapped his cracked ribs. He'd groaned quite a bit, but not once did he open his eyes. The doctor told them it was normal for him to sleep a lot after what his body had been through, but the nurses continued to disturb him on the hour to be sure he wouldn't slip into a coma.

On the ride to their farm, Lydia carried on nervous small talk with Lucy about shucking corn and shelling peas. They talked about the upcoming canning bee that the women of the community would begin soon. They even discussed the excitement over the quilt shop and the plans for it once the renovations were completed. Lydia kept the conversation going as much as she could to avoid thinking about Steve, who was pressed quite close to her in the small cab of his truck. She had become smitten with Steve the first time she'd met him, and she secretly hoped he liked her too.

Since Liam had left home, Lydia had not been afforded the opportunity to have a serious beau. She was always too busy doing Liam's old chores along with her own, and most her *mamm's* usual duties. She too was overworked and overtired most days to even think about having a beau. But now, as she snuggled close to Steve, she was all too aware of what she'd been missing out on when each of her friends had gotten married one-by-one. Lucy was the only friend she had left that was still single, and the two of them threw themselves into their work to avoid the obvious emptiness they each endured on a daily basis.

Lydia had advised Lucy many years ago to stop waiting for her *bruder* to return, but the poor thing hadn't listened to her. Today, she saw the love in Lucy's eyes when they were in Liam's hospital room, and the light in her eyes had returned. Lucy had appeared happy, but Lydia could still see reservation in her expression. She imagined it had to have been tough for Lucy to pretend with Liam that they were still young, especially since that was the time in their lives when they were in love.

Chattering on, Lydia was grateful that Lucy was easy to talk to. Her *bruder* had been a fool to leave Lucy, but Lydia was content with their friendship. Their common bond had been their abandonment from Liam. It had in some ways brought them together as friends, but Lydia often wondered if their friendship was a bit strained by the pain Lucy felt in her presence at times.

Holidays had been especially difficult for all of them. When Lucy brought a gift for Lydia each year on her birthday, Lydia could tell that thoughts of Liam were in the back of Lucy's mind. Lydia knew that whatever the outcome of this new set of circumstances, they would have each other to lean on if things became tough.

They both avoided the obvious during their chatter; neither of them wanted to admit that Liam's memory lapse could actually be a blessing in disguise. Even Nellie had seemed a little curious to know how the situation could work in their favor. They were all eager to see Liam heal, but they also didn't mind the possibility that this could bring the outcome they'd all hoped for along the past seven years.

Lucy shifted in her seat and leaned against the door of the truck, watching mindlessly as the landscaping coasted by in a blur of color. Barns blended with trees and cows seemed an extension of the earth. Was Lydia going to talk the entire way home? Lucy tried politely to tune out her nervous prattling, but the girl just kept engaging her in question after question. If she knew Lydia, she was using conversation to cover up something that was weighing on her mind. Lucy had her own issues she was trying not to think about, but it was no use trying to push them down because they seemed to repeatedly surface on their own.

Lucy let her mind drift to Liam, and wondered how long it would be before he realized he didn't really love her anymore. No amount of pretending could make him love her if didn't, especially if the memories he relied on were from a time when he *did* love her. Those old feelings might be better left in the past, but Lucy couldn't push them down any longer.

How could Liam forget that he wasn't in love with her anymore? Was it possible that he'd never stopped loving her, and the accident had brought *his* feelings to the surface? The only question that still plagued Lucy was whether or not Liam had loved any other woman in the time they'd been apart. If he had, was there any real hope for them to reconcile? Was Lucy capable of forgiving such an offense, or would she spend the rest of their lives letting it eat away at her until she became so bitter that she could no longer love him? She prayed it wasn't so.

Chapter 22

"At least let me send you home with a jar of my homemade apple butter."

There was a gentle insistence in Lydia's tone that Steve could not resist.

"That sounds wonderful, thank you. I'll wait right here."

Steve knew better than to accept the invite from Lydia for a glass of iced tea on the porch. So he sat in the truck and watched Lucy disappear into the cornfield that separated her farm from Lydia's. Even though it was dusk, he could see that a wide trail had been left between the tall rows of corn. He guessed it was planted that way on purpose to allow passage between the two farms. It intrigued him how neighborly the Amish were. He'd lived that way growing up, being on a street where all the neighbors pitched in to help one another. He missed that now that he lived in the city.

Steve rolled down the window of his truck so he could listen to the crickets. The wind rustled the tassels on the corn stalks, bringing him out of his truck to get a better listen to the country sounds that captivated his attention. He was so absorbed in the charm of the land that he didn't hear Lydia step out of the front door of the farm house. A light flickered to the side of him as Lydia lit the lantern on the small table on the porch. When she beckoned him onto the porch, he resisted only for a minute. His better judgment told him Liam wouldn't approve, but Lydia's eyes hypnotized his heart just long enough to reel him in. He sat in one of the wooden chairs separated by the table that housed the lantern and the tray of iced tea that Lydia had brought out for them to share.

"I hope you don't find it too presumptuous, but when I saw you get out of your truck to admire the corn, I thought you changed your mind about joining me for a refreshing sip of iced tea."

Steve nodded to her, watching her pour the tea into tall glasses filled with slices of lemon. Soft blond tendrils fluttered against her cheek, and her eyes shone like the stars that were just beginning to light up the indigo sky. He was mesmerized by her beauty that didn't come from makeup or fancy hair or clothing like the city girls. Lydia's beauty came from within and radiated to her outer appearance like a halo. To Steve, she was the most beautiful woman he'd ever laid eyes on.

"Just a half glass for me," he said, interrupting her pouring. "Then I should be on my way. I'm not sure your brother would approve of me being here without an escort."

Lydia paused before setting the pitcher of tea back on the small table. "I'm a grown woman, and *mei bruder* hasn't been here to guide me in that process, so I'm not sure he has claim to his say about the matter."

Steve had been awkward at dating since he was a teenager. He was shy and didn't know what to say half the time, but Lydia had put him at ease from the moment he'd met her. Her smile was enough to melt his pounding heart.

"I imagine he would have a lot to say. He's still your brother, and he's never stopped loving you. I've heard so much about you over the years, I feel like I already know you."

Lydia nearly choked on her iced tea. "That hardly seems fair! You'll have to catch me up so I know an equal amount about you."

Steve cleared his throat. "That could take a while."

"The only thing I have to do right now is watch the corn grow." Lydia smiled at him.

Steve relaxed a little and smiled back. If Lydia was okay with him sitting on the porch alone with her, then he wouldn't argue. He was happy to be in her company, and Liam had all but given him his blessing earlier—before the accident.

"You know I met your brother back in ninth grade. He still lived at home back then, and it was a struggle for him. If not for the support of his dad, he wouldn't have made it to graduation."

Lydia's eyes grew wide. "I didn't know our *daed* knew he was going to the public school."

"Your dad was supposed to go to Liam's graduation, but he…didn't make it."

"Because he died in the accident," Lydia added.

"Yes," Steve said quietly. "Liam told me he was going to bring your mother to the graduation."

"*Mamm* knew about it too?" Lydia was having a hard time grasping that bit of information. "Why didn't she tell me?"

Steve didn't know what to say. He didn't want to be in the middle of this conversation or in the middle of the feud between sister and brother.

"I've found over the years that sometimes people have a tough time telling others how they really feel about things. From what I know of your brother, I'd say you all need to learn to communicate a little better. And don't think I haven't said that to *him* quite a lot since I've known him."

Lydia sighed. "Maybe Liam's accident was a blessing in disguise. Maybe now that he thinks he's back where all this started, we can have a chance to work through what went so wrong in our *familye* after *mei daed's* accident. None of us spoke to each other after the accident; we just held in our feelings about everything and went our own separate ways."

Lydia pondered her own statement as she gazed up into the sea of stars against a cobalt sky. The crescent moon hung amidst the stars as though keeping order over the vast universe. She listened to the crickets and the rustling of the corn stalks in the field as if the resonance whispered a message of hope directly from *Gott*—as if hope floated across the warm, summer breeze.

Chapter 23

Lucy stepped onto the path between the rows of corn that led to Lydia's farm. Though the sun had barely tipped over the horizon, she was to meet Lydia so the two of them could get a ride into town with Steve. She hadn't told her folks she was going to the hospital again or anything about Liam's accident because they would not understand her need to be involved. Her *familye* had lectured her repeatedly about letting go of Liam, but she had not let her heart let go of him. Now she was on her way to the hospital to see him, and she felt as nervous as a teenager again.

Reaching out a hand, Lucy tapped the leaves of the cornstalks as she whisked by them. Liam used to chase her around this very field in the summers, and they would swim in Goose Pond, and skate across it in the winter. She had a history with Liam, and now she had a chance at the future with him she'd always dreamed of. Even though it wasn't the ideal beginning to that future, she was determined to try to make it work to her advantage. She'd missed him more than she realized.

Suppressing a yawn, Lucy pressed on though the dirt under her feet was still very damp with early morning dew. She hadn't slept much, and thought about the thermos of coffee she carried, wondering if it would be enough to keep her awake all day. She'd been so consumed with thoughts of Liam, she hadn't fallen asleep until well into the wee hours. At eight o'clock now, she'd been up for two hours already doing chores to prepare for her absence from the farm for the day.

All she could think about the entire night was how she felt about leaving her *familye* and the community to cling to Liam. She was more mature than she was the first time she'd pondered the question, and she believed more than ever that she was finally ready. If that was what Liam would require of her, she would choose *him* this time. She loved him; she had never stopped.

At the clearing, Lucy could see Steve's work truck parked in front of Lydia's *haus.* Steve leaned up against the bed of the truck, his hands moving around tools in the back. The squeak of the screen door let Lucy know that Lydia had been waiting for her approach before exiting the *haus.* In her arms was a medium rucksack, and if she knew Lydia, it was packed with food for the day. Lucy hadn't thought past the thermos of coffee that she hoped would keep her awake. With food in her belly, it might be tough to fight sleep with the long day ahead of her.

After a brief greeting, she and Lydia climbed into the truck and they headed toward the hospital. The closer they got, the more Lucy's stomach roiled with second thoughts. She was so sure she'd made the right decision, but now that she was about to come face-to-face with Liam, she began to overanalyze her decision yet again.

Thankfully, Lydia didn't seem to be in a very chatty mood this morning, or Lucy would not have been able to sort out her feelings before they reached the hospital. Secure in her resolve, Lucy stepped out of the truck with confidence in knowing exactly how she would handle herself with Liam when she saw him.

Lydia already noticed a connection with Steve. Their long talk the night before had helped bring them closer together, and she was content with their friendship moving at such a fast pace. At twenty-five, Lydia was at risk of becoming a spinster according to the way most Amish viewed marriage. Most girls are married by the time they turn twenty, and Lydia had watched each of her friends marry. There was not much choice of bachelors in the community, but Lydia did not care. Her heart was already filling with hope for a future with Steve. Though she feared her *mamm* would not approve, she tried to push the thought of leaving the community the way Liam had out of her mind for the time-being. Was she prepared to leave if forced to choose? There was a part of her that was, and that frightened her enough to push down the thoughts.

Lydia took her time scooting out of the middle of the cab of the truck, enjoying the feel of the hand Steve had offered her. In her opinion, it fit perfectly. The only thing that could be more pleasant would be to have his lips meet hers. Now was not the time for that, Lydia knew, but that didn't stop her from daydreaming about that perfect moment when such a magical thing would finally happen for her. One look into Steve's blue eyes, and Lydia was certain he was thinking the same thing. She'd caught him gazing at her mouth a few times last night, and she'd hoped he would be assertive enough to give into the temptation, but he hadn't. Much to her dismay, he'd acted like the perfect gentleman.

With Lucy already ducking into the hospital entrance ahead of them, Lydia was tempted to linger outside with Steve for a few moments, but she knew her *mamm* would need the change of clothing she'd brought for her. She'd also brought a pair of her *daed's* trousers and a shirt just like her *mamm* had asked of her because Liam's clothes he'd left behind in his teens would no longer fit him. Lydia wished she'd had the time to wash the musty clothes she'd taken from the old trunk in the attic, but they would have to do for now.

Lydia and Steve ambled down the hallway to Liam's room. It was evident to her that Steve enjoyed her company, and she hoped that when Liam was well, she and Steve would have the opportunity to explore those feelings a little more in-depth. For now, she would concentrate on helping her *bruder* get back to whatever path he would take for his life. Liam had been given a fresh start whether he was aware of it yet or not, and Lydia would do everything she could to make sure she and her *mamm* were a part of his future.

Chapter 24

Lucy crept quietly into Liam's room, careful not to disturb him. She'd run into Nellie at the nurse's station, and the woman encouraged Lucy to take a turn visiting with her son while she stretched her legs.

Grateful for a few moments of privacy with Liam, Lucy sat in the chair beside the bed and pulled his hand into hers. Even in the hospital gown, Liam was adorable. She longed for him to wake so she could pull him into her arms and declare her love for him, but there would be plenty of time for that later. For now, she would be content that he had survived the accident, and that *Gott* had given them all a second chance with him.

Liam turned his head toward Lucy and opened his eyes a small slit. His vision was still blurry, but he could feel the warmth of her hand in his. He groaned as he tried to move. His ribs hurt and his head pounded.

"Don't try to get up," Lucy's gentle voice urged. "You've had an accident. Do you remember anything yet?"

He winced from the pain in his head. "The buggy accident!"

Liam tried to sit up again, but was unable due to the pain coursing through him. "Is *mei daed* here too? Is he injured?"

Tears constricted Lucy's throat. How could she tell the *mann* she loved that his *daed* had passed away seven years before?

Nellie walked into the room just then and stood at her son's bedside.

"Your *daed* is not here, Liam. He's visiting relatives."

It was enough to calm him down, but both women knew it wouldn't satisfy him for long. It wasn't exactly a lie, Nellie conveniently left out the part about it being relatives in Heaven that her husband was with. The two women looked at each other for a long moment, stress distorting their faces. They knew the real explanation would come out soon enough, but for now, Liam was content.

Unable to control her tears, Lucy excused herself abruptly and exited the room. In the hall, she let her tears flow freely. What had she been thinking when she'd decided that reuniting with Liam was a *gut* idea? It hadn't really sunk in that she would have to pretend to be seventeen again in order to keep him. What if he never regained his memory of the last seven years? Would she have to pretend to have her birthdays all over again? She'd wished so many times to have those years back, but now that she was faced with it, the concept was a little too terrifying for her to deal with.

She felt a hand on her shuddering shoulders and immediately stiffened and wiped her face. Nellie pulled Lucy into her arms allowing her to let go of a fresh batch of tears.

"I'm so sorry," Lucy sobbed. "I didn't know what to say to him when he asked me about—your husband."

"You've done a fine job of caring for him during this. I'm happy he had you here with him yesterday before I was able to get here. Thank you for helping us. You don't have to be here, but I know you are here because you love him, and I'm grateful my son has you to care for him. I've prayed that *Gott* will give the two of you another chance to make things right between you."

"Thank you," Lucy said quietly.

Lydia and Steve met them in the hall. Nellie and Lydia exchanged a strained glance between them before she handed her *mamm* the bag in her hand.

"I brought you a spare dress and *Daed's* clothing for Liam so he can wear them home tomorrow."

Lucy turned her gaze sharply until it met Nellie's. "You're bringing Liam *home* with *you?"*

"*Jah.* The doctor here said it's best if he follows a normal routine and remains in familiar surroundings to trigger his memories."

Lucy's head filled with immediate questions, but she didn't want to be disrespectful to Nellie.

Steve spoke the words she'd been thinking but didn't dare utter. "He should probably go back to his apartment in the South Bend. That would probably trigger his memories faster, wouldn't you think?"

"*Nee.* He believes he's still a teen, and it might be traumatic for him to find out suddenly that he'd left the community. As long as he believes his *daed* to be still alive, he needs to be at home with me and his *schweschder,* so that when his memory comes back, we will be there to comfort him through it."

Steve nodded. "That makes sense."

Lucy couldn't hold it in any longer. "He thinks he was in the buggy accident with his *daed.* He asked me about it just before you walked in the room."

Nellie sighed. "Then I suppose we will have to break the news to him a little bit at a time. We can start by taking him by the quilt shop in a few days and showing him what really happened. Maybe that will trigger something in his mind. He's going to expect to try to finish school, so Steve, you're going to have to come up with a reason he doesn't need to go anymore."

Steve nodded. "What if we just tell him that a little time has passed and he already graduated?"

"I don't want to confuse him more, but the doctor did say he needs to be brought up to the present time—but slowly. Maybe if we tell him everything a little at a time, he will come to it on his own."

They all agreed, but Lucy still had a few reservations. If he regained his memory too quickly, she feared he would remember he no longer loved her, and it would destroy their chance at a future together.

Chapter 25

Liam couldn't shake the feeling that nagged him about his apprehension over going home with his *mamm* and Lydia. He couldn't put his finger on it, but something seemed a little off about the situation. Despite reassurance from the doctors, his *familye,* and Steve, his best friend, he still felt uneasiness creeping into his mind. Was there something that his *familye* was keeping from him? Why had his *daed* taken this opportunity to visit with his relatives? Hadn't he been in the buggy accident with Liam?

Pieces of his memories were missing, and it troubled Liam to the point of exhaustion. The doctors had advised him not to try too hard to remember, reassuring him the memories would return on their own. But what if they never did? What if he never remembered what happened to him? Would it be that bad? Maybe it was better that he didn't remember his accident. But he couldn't shake the feeling everyone was keeping something important from him.

Liam had his whole life ahead of him, and Lucy had agreed to marry him and start a new life with him outside of the Amish community. It had been his dream to have his own construction business, with his best friend working side-by-side, and now it was closer than ever. All he had to do was finish his last few weeks of school and graduate, and then he would be eighteen and ready to be on his own—with Lucy, the love of his life.

Lucy and Lydia had remained at the Yoder farm that morning to prepare for Liam's homecoming. No matter how hard Lucy tried to stay calm, the butterflies disturbed her stomach. Why had she agreed to run off with Liam? Would he expect her to if he didn't regain his memory before he was able to leave the community? She knew he had at the very least a week of physical recovery ahead of him, but would that prevent him from pushing her to make plans with him? She wondered what would happen when he realized he already had a place of his own in the city.

Lucy pulled fresh muffins from the oven and upturned them into a linen-lined basket. Lydia had practically begged her to make them since they had always been Liam's favorites. She couldn't deny him that; she would do anything for him. Even carrying on the charade of reliving their youth was all for him—or was it? She had to admit that a part of her felt selfish for wanting another chance with Liam, even it meant he might not remember they had been split up for so long.

"Do you fear that Liam will leave us all over again when he remembers what happened and how much time has really passed?"

Lydia's question startled Lucy, who'd been lost in her own thoughts. It was a legitimate question, and one that warranted an answer, but Lucy couldn't allow herself to think about the consequences of the situation. The entire thing could backfire in their faces, but to Lucy, it was worth a try just to be near the *mann* she loved once again.

"Let's not borrow trouble, Lydia. We should remain strong in our faith and believe that the outcome will be *Gotte's Wille.*"

The very thought of leaving her future up to *Gott* terrified Lucy. She knew better than to let her faith waver, but she did not have the strength to recover from another heartbreak involving Liam, and she suspected the same was true for Lydia and Nellie.

Lydia smiled at her friend. "You're right. They will be here soon. Is there anything we forgot?"

Lucy took a mental note of all the breakfast foods that spread across the table and hoped Liam would have an appetite when he walked in and smelled the food. No sooner had she resolved they hadn't missed anything, than they heard Steve's truck pull into the drive at the back of the *haus*.

Lydia and Lucy stared at each other wide-eyed for a brief moment before busying themselves with setting the dishes on the table. Steve entered through the kitchen door with Liam leaning on him for support. Lucy pulled out a kitchen chair just in time for Steve to lower Liam into it. Groaning from the pain, Liam took a few deep breaths. Lucy rushed to the sink and wet a linen dishtowel and brought it to him, mopping up the sweat on his brow. Liam clasped his hand over hers and held the linen towel over his eyes. His hand shook as he breathed in deeply, but he didn't let go of Lucy's hand.

Feeling awkward, Lucy pulled gently to release her hand from his. "I hope you're hungry; we made you some breakfast."

"It smells *gut.* I didn't eat much at the hospital because it didn't taste like *mamm's* cooking." He removed the cloth from his eyes and pointed his blurry gaze in Nellie's direction. "Where's *Daed?* I was hoping he'd be back by now. I need to talk to him."

Silence suffocated the room.

Nellie bravely stepped forward and placed a hand on her son's shoulder. "Is it something that can wait, or can I help instead?"

"Nee. It can wait. Let's eat. I'm starving."

Lucy eyed Liam for a moment. Was it just her imagination, or had his last few sentences sounded more like an *Englischer*? If he was speaking differently, then it was possible his brain was beginning to heal, and it was only a matter of time before he realized he was no longer in love with her. Would she lose him forever, or would she have enough time to make him fall in love with her all over again? Lucy had to face the possibility that her plan might not work, and that terrified her.

Chapter 26

Lydia sat on the front porch once again with Steve. With her *mamm* and Lucy preoccupied with her *bruder,* Lydia intended to take advantage of a little time for herself to see where her new friendship with Steve would take them. He'd been invited for dinner after a long day at the quilt shop working on the renovation, and Lydia was glad for the private time they could spend getting to know one another.

Lighting the citronella buckets Steve had brought her from the hardware store in town, Lydia was grateful for his consideration in keeping away the mosquitoes. The night before when they'd sat out here, she'd gotten bitten a few times.

"It's very humid tonight," Steve said. "The mosquitoes like the humidity. Hopefully once those candles burn for a few minutes, they'll disappear and we can enjoy the night breeze again."

Lydia poured two tall glasses of iced tea, hoping the refreshing brew would keep them cool enough to sit for a while.

"How did your day go at the quilt shop?"

Steve sighed. "I'll admit it wasn't the same without your brother, but I think we managed to keep anymore of the ceiling from caving in. I think we have it all secure now. We don't need anyone else getting hurt. Liam seemed a little more alert at dinner."

"Jah, I think he got a lot of rest today. Maybe sleeping in his own bed again made him feel better."

"I don't blame him. It's peaceful out here. I wouldn't mind settling down in a place like this myself."

Lydia felt her heart leap against her ribcage. Was it possible her way of life was appealing enough to Steve that he would consider marrying her some day? She knew it was too soon to think such things, but she couldn't help it. She was smitten with Steve, and it seemed he was beginning to show signs he was thinking along the same path as she was.

"Most people like it better here than in the city. You can see every star out here without the city lights blocking them out. The city is much too noisy and busy."

Steve stood up and offered his hand to her.

"Let's take a look at those stars, shall we?"

Lydia felt giddiness try to overcome her as she placed her hand in Steve's and allowed him to guide her down the steps of the porch. Their hands remained clenched as they walked along the path toward the cornfield away from the canopy of trees that blocked out the sky.

Steve stopped just short of the entrance to the cornfield and turned to face Lydia. He wanted to kiss her with everything that was in him, but he put his emotions in check for fear he might be pushing things along too quickly for Lydia's comfort.

It was Lydia who closed the space between them. Now that she stood dangerously close to Steve, he couldn't resist leaning down and touching his lips to hers.

Lucy breathed a sigh of relief when Nellie excused herself to retire for the night. She hadn't been alone with Liam since the day of his accident, and she was eager to spend some quality time with him. She knew she couldn't stay long because he needed his rest, but she was not ready to let him go so easily just yet. She stared at his handsome face in the glow of the lantern light that illuminated the room.

Liam smiled. "I can't believe *mamm* left us alone like this. But it doesn't matter because we will be married soon and we will have our own place in the city."

"It sounds wonderful!"

"When we become *Englischers* we will have to talk the way they do if we want to fit in. We will have to dress like them too. Are you going to be able to do that, Lucy?"

Lucy swallowed hard. She hadn't thought that far ahead. Was she willing to give up her plain clothing for clothing that wasn't modest? For Liam, she would if it meant keeping him in her life.

"*Jah.* I mean, *yes.*"

"I haven't told *mamm* about our plans yet. I was hoping to talk to *mei daed* first. I wish she would tell me when he's expected to return from his trip."

Lucy suppressed the tears that threatened to spill from her eyes, and was grateful the wick in the lantern had burned down enough to dim the room, allowing her to better hide her feelings.

"Have you decided where you want us to live?"

Lucy tried changing the subject, hoping Liam would take the bait.

Liam pushed his hand through his hair. "I had planned on getting a place with Steve, but now that you've agreed to marry me, I guess we'll have to find our own place. I have enough money saved to get us started, but I'll have to find work right away."

He ran his fingers through his hair again, feeling puzzled. "Why is my hair so short? Did they have to cut it because of the stitches in my head?"

How could she answer that without lying to him? "You are the one who cut it," she blurted out without thinking through her answer.

He slowly sat up, wincing as he maneuvered into an upright position. "Why did I cut it? To look more *Englisch?"*

"Jah."

It was all she could say, but it was the truth.

"I don't want you to cut your hair," Liam said as he pulled her by her hands until she sat at the edge of his bed.

Lucy reached up and unpinned her *kapp* and set it on the bedside table. She used to pull her hair down for him all the time when they were dating, but did she dare do it now, after all these years? To him, time had not moved forward seven years, but for her, it seemed almost too much time had passed since she'd held him in her arms.

Chapter 27

Lucy woke a little later than usual feeling disappointed that she wouldn't have more than a few minutes to see Liam when she went to pick up Lydia to drive into town. Since Nellie would be staying at home caring for Liam for the next few days, Lydia offered to oversee the renovations of the quilt shop. Lucy knew the main reason she'd volunteered was so she could see Steve, but Lucy would never dream of exposing her friend's secret "crush".

Just as the sun began to show, streaking pinks and yellows across the horizon, Lucy pulled her buggy into the back side of the Yoder farm. She stepped down onto the dew-drenched grass and walked sleepily up the steps to the kitchen door. She knocked a brief warning before entering. The smell of freshly fried bacon and cinnamon rolls filled her senses. She'd left home without any breakfast, eager to get to the bakery after leaving it closed for the past two days. Her regular customers would be lined outside the door waiting on her this morning, she was sure of it, and she knew she was in for a long day. The sooner she arrived, the sooner she could be done and return to Liam at the end of her day.

Lydia was still sitting at the table, and quickly shoved the last piece of bacon in her mouth. Lucy had to smile at her friend, who could eat twice as much as she could and never gain an ounce. Lucy, on the other hand, had grown a little thicker over the past few years, and had often wondered if it was one of the reasons she was still single. It was something she had worried about when she saw Liam again for the first time after so many years, but thankfully, he'd acted like he hadn't even noticed.

"Sit and have some food. I made too much as usual."

Lucy waved her off. "*Nee.* If I'm to make a *gut* impression on your *bruder,* I need to start watching what I eat. It doesn't help that I have a habit of tasting a sample from each batch of pastries at the bakery."

"You are skin and bones, Lucy! Eat!"

Lucy didn't believe her, but she had to admit she was very hungry. She agreed to a little bit of eggs and one piece of bacon. Liam entered the room clutching his ribs just then and caused Lucy to spit eggs into her napkin. Why was she suddenly so nervous around him? They'd spent a pleasant evening together, and had even made plans for their future.

"Lydia's right. I've always thought you were too thin, Lucy. Stay for a few minutes and eat with me."

Liam smiled, and Lucy jumped up nervously to fill a plate for him. She set it front of him, feeling self-conscious about eating, so she took small bites, while Liam gobbled his food and asked for a second helping.

After a little bit of small-talk, Lydia came back into the kitchen and asked if Lucy was ready. Lucy wasn't ready to go; she wanted to stay and have things be as magical as they had been the night before, but she could sense something had changed in Liam. Was it possible that he'd remembered his real life, and he no longer wanted anything to do with her? Lucy suddenly felt like a fraud, and hoped he wouldn't end up hating her instead.

Liam wiped his mouth and tossed the linen napkin carelessly on his plate. "Where are the two of you off to today?"

The two women eyed each other for a moment, and Lucy wondered if they should tell him the truth. At his present memory level, Liam would have no idea about her bakery, since her *daed* did not present her with it until Liam had already left the community. He certainly had no recollection that his *mamm* now owned a quilt shop.

"We have a few things to take care of in town," Lydia offered. "We will be gone most of the day, but I will be back in time to help *mamm* prepare the evening meal."

Liam looked at the two of them as though he knew they were keeping something from him. "What business do the two of have in town that would keep you all day?"

He turned his attention toward Lucy. "Are you going to the bakery?"

Lucy's heart slammed against her ribcage. If he knew about the bakery, then he must remember that they were no longer together.

"*Jah.* How did you know?" she was almost too afraid to ask.

"Your *daed* gave it to you for your eighteenth birthday. But you're birthday isn't for a few more…weeks."

Lucy looked into Liam's confused expression and couldn't help but fear that he would remember at any moment that he no longer loved her, and her future with him would be over—again. Lydia tried to nudge her out the kitchen door, but Lucy's feet felt like they were nailed to the floor. Silence hovered between them until Nellie entered the room.

"You two better get going or you'll be late opening that bakery," she said sternly.

Liam turned to his *mamm.* "Have I missed something?"

Nellie shooed the girls with her hand, though they both looked worried—Lucy more than Lydia.

"You haven't missed anything. The doctor told you that you had a few things missing from your memory, but it will all come back to you in time."

"I think I'm going to head out to the barn and feed Buttercup. The doctor said the sooner I get back to my normal routine the easier I will start to remember the little things I'm missing." Liam stood up slowly.

Nellie put a hand on his shoulder. How could she tell him that his old mare had died a few years back? "You can't tend to Buttercup because you're *daed* took the horse with him."

Chapter 28

Lydia pushed Lucy out the kitchen door. She couldn't stand to be in the *haus* with her *bruder* another minute. How could her *mamm* be so casual about the dead horse, or about their dead father for that matter? Lydia knew she could never be that brave for Liam's sake. What was her *mamm* thinking telling Liam such a thing?

Lydia burst out laughing.

Lucy looked at her friend as though she'd gone mad. "What is so funny?"

Lydia could barely stop laughing long enough to answer her. "The horse is dead! And *Mamm* told Liam that *mei daed* took the horse with him!"

Lucy stifled a giggle. "It's not funny."

"I know it's not," she said. "But in a way it is."

Lucy crinkled her brow. "This is like when we were young and our *mamm's* told us to behave during Sunday service, and you know you aren't supposed to laugh, but you can't help it, so you laugh when it's inappropriate to laugh."

Lydia giggled some more. "That's it exactly!"

Lucy suppressed another giggle. "Liam isn't going to be too happy with your *mamm* when he finds out what *really* happened to that horse."

"Buttercup had a happy life, but she was very old. He knew that when he left. He knew she wouldn't last much longer, and he couldn't face it, just like he couldn't face the death of our *daed.*"

The conversation took a sudden serious turn, and Lucy didn't want to discuss it. Thinking of all the things Liam would have rushing to his memory of the past few years scared Lucy to her very soul. He would feel betrayed by her when he remembered they were no longer in love. Would he despise her for lying to him, or would he realize she'd done it to spare him additional grief?

Lucy walked toward the buggy, feeling like she was suffocating. She placed a hand to her heaving chest, willing herself to breathe in slowly so she wouldn't pass out. She knew her fragile heart couldn't take the pressure of being broken by Liam a second time, but she had to keep calm in front of Lydia. She was certain that when Liam remembered she'd rejected him all those years ago he would never let her back into his life. She didn't want to appear rude to Lydia, but she was in no shape emotionally to be discussing this any further.

"Wait for me, Lucy," Lydia called after her.

Lydia climbed into the buggy just in time before Lucy slapped the reins lightly against her mare. The horse trotted off down the long drive to the main road, while the two of them sat in silence.

Lydia put a hand on Lucy's arm. "I'm sorry. All this talk of Liam's memory must be upsetting you."

Lucy swallowed tears that felt as though they were choking her. "I'm afraid that if your *bruder* remembers we were apart all these years that he will leave me all over again. I don't know if I can handle the heartbreak a second time."

"I've seen the genuine love in his eyes when he looks at you. It's the same way he used to look at you when you were younger."

Lucy wiped away a tear. "That's because he thinks we are back there at that time in our lives. If he knew how things were between us now, he wouldn't look at me like that."

Lydia took the reins so Lucy could blow her nose. "Love like that doesn't go away so easily. You haven't stopped loving him after all these years. Perhaps it is the same for him."

Lucy tucked the handkerchief in her apron pocket. "I've been a fool to hope he'd come back to me after all this time."

"*Nee.* True love endures forever," Lydia said, trying to comfort her.

Lucy could not calm her galloping heart no matter how many slow, deep breaths she took in. Her nerves were twisted in knots, and her stomach roiled, making her wish she hadn't eaten.

"Maybe ours was not true love," Lucy cleared her throat to control the tears that made her voice squeaky, but it was no use. "That is why we are no longer together."

Lydia huffed. "You're no longer together because *mei bruder* has acted like a fool."

Lucy could see past the anger that twisted Lydia's face. She loved her *bruder,* but she was pledging loyalty to her friend. Lucy didn't want her to feel as though she should choose sides. Lydia was free to care about both of them, although Lucy had to admit it was nice to have a confidante.

"He did act very much like a fool," Lucy agreed. "But so did I. We were both too young to be making the kind of decisions he wanted us to make. Not to mention, he didn't give me more than a few minutes to think about it. Maybe if we had talked about it before he made up his mind, I could have helped him through whatever he was going through at the time."

Lydia shook her head. "*Nee,* he had to figure this out for himself. All you can do now is continue to love him and hope that when he remembers, he'll see that you stood by him all this time and appreciate you more for it."

"I pray that you are right, Lydia."

Lucy was tired of analyzing the whole thing. She knew the only way to really know if she was doing the right thing would be to jump in with both feet and hope for the best. She was in it for the long term, and she prayed Liam would see that when he regained his memory. If he didn't, then she had to prepare herself to walk away and move on with her life. She was certain she would never stop loving Liam, and prayed it was so for him too, but her heart would probably never let him go. She would remain devoted to him for as long as he would have her.

Chapter 29

Two days had passed, and Lucy had watched Lydia and Steve develop their friendship into something more, while she and Liam seemed to be at an impasse. All day at work, Lucy could hear Lydia and Steve talking and laughing while they worked on the quilt shop. They had made considerable progress, and the *menner* that worked for Liam had already installed the new ceiling. It was starting to look like a shop finally, and Lucy hoped Liam would be pleased with the work they had done in his absence. That is if he would ever remember his present life.

Lucy still couldn't be certain she wanted Liam to regain his memory, but it seemed things between them were a little strained. Maybe it was just her insecurities playing tricks on her, but she'd hoped things would progress between them a little faster. He was healing physically quite fast, but his spirit seemed a little sluggish, and that worried Lucy. She loved him more than anything, and wanted to be the one he would lean on, to be the one to make all of his pain go away, but she just didn't know him anymore.

When Lucy approached the clearing in the cornfield, Liam stood there waiting for her. His appearance startled her a little.

"You're up out of bed! Did Doctor Davis give you an exam today?"

Liam gently tugged on her hand, pulling her into the open yard. "He says I'm healing nicely, and it should only be a few more days before I can get back to work doing easy stuff—but no lifting for another week."

"*Das gut.* I hope your head is feeling better. How about your vision?"

She had to admit she was still a little nervous about having Liam see how she looked now. She felt so old suddenly, and very plain, and hoped he wouldn't dislike what he saw in her. She knew vanity was wrong, but she just couldn't push down the worries.

"Vision is improving, but I might still need a little help making my way around."

He patted her hand lovingly and tucked it into the crook of his elbow, escorting her instead of the other way around. She wondered if he was using his blurry vision as an excuse to be nearer to her, but she didn't care. She was happy for the closeness.

"Would you like to sit on the porch? I can go inside and bring out some tea or lemonade—whatever your *mamm* might have in the kitchen to drink."

He tugged her in the opposite direction. "I'm not thirsty; I'd rather take a walk down to the pond if that's alright with you. If I remember correctly, it's one of our favorite spots."

If he remembered correctly? What did he mean by that?

When they reached the edge of the pond, he didn't release her hand where it was tucked neatly in the crook of his arm. Lucy gazed upon the moonlit water as she took in the sounds of frogs singing to one another across the glass-like surface of the pond. Crickets chirped in the tall grasses to either side of the dock, and an occasional bird sent out a call to another, where an answer would come from a nearby tree. Lucy wasn't sure how long she could endure the distraction of nature that seemed to grow louder the more anxious she became. She had to break the silence, but what should she say?

"This pond hasn't changed one bit." He covered her hand with his free hand and gave it a squeeze.

Before she had a chance to think about it, he turned to her and pulled her close. "I've never stopped loving you, Lucy. You are the love of my life."

Lucy felt tormented. She wanted to lean into the strong plane of his chest and lose herself in the folds of his arms. Her conscience would not allow her to lie to him; she was compelled to tell him the truth no matter how much it hurt them both.

"You're not mine anymore…"

Liam interrupted her as his lips met hers. His soft mouth swept over hers making her hunger for more. She couldn't break from him even if she wanted to. Her will to do what was right became clouded in the delight of his lips against hers, making it impossible for her to think clearly. The sounds of the crickets and frogs became like delicate music in her ears, when only moments ago it had begun to annoy her. Suddenly everything felt right as a love so powerful surged through her, a love unbreakable by time or distance. Nothing would ever be the same for her again.

Liam couldn't resist Lucy's magnetic force pulling him further into the kiss. She smelled like baking spices and sugar, something he would cherish forever. He saw his future in the blue of her eyes, a future he could not bear without her tucked neatly at his side.

His mouth trailed to her cheek and toward her temple where he whispered his unwavering love for her. She would be his, and his world would be right again no matter what it took to make it so.

"I have never stopped loving you, and I want to spend the rest of my life proving it to you."

Regret would not overtake him for time lost between them, for he intended to make up for every day they'd lost over the past seven years.

She pulled away gently. "You remember, don't you?"

Liam sank to one knee in front of her, trying not to wince from the pain in his ribs. He swept his hand in hers and pulled it to his lips, allowing it to linger there for just enough time for her to catch her breath.

"I remember nearly all of it. There are still a few things that are a little fuzzy, but I remember how much I hurt you when I left here seven years ago, and I promise you I never intend to hurt you again. Please, Lucy, marry me so I can spend the rest of my days proving to you just how much I love you."

Tears constricted Lucy's throat. Was this really happening to her? Was this handsome *mann* she had loved since they were mere children really kneeling before her asking for her hand in marriage? She could see the sincerity in his eyes that pooled with the moisture of his emotion.

"*Jah,* I mean yes! I will marry you."

Liam stood faster than he should have and scooped Lucy into his arms, ignoring the pain in his ribs. His lips met hers again, and she leaned into the kiss, deepening it with all the love she felt for him.

With those three simple words, Liam had brought years of worry and angst to an end for Lucy. Her wait was finally over, and her future was about to begin with the *mann* she'd loved since they were both young. Her future was finally secure, and she would never again have to wonder if he still loved her or what could have been between them, because he was very much in love with her, and they were going to spend the rest of their lives together.

Chapter 30

Liam had no idea how he would break the news to his mother that he'd regained his memory. She'd gone to such great lengths to shelter him from the news of his father's death, and that of his favorite horse, that he didn't have the heart to hurt her again.

But tell her he must.

He'd enjoyed the last week with her and Lydia, and didn't want to break the bond they'd revisited. His love for them was steadfast, and they needed to know he regretted the decisions he'd made as a foolish youth. He intended to make up for lost time with his family as well as Lucy, but he wasn't certain how to approach the subject. He'd always jumped in feet first, but he was an adult now, and needed to control his impulsive nature to spare his mother and sister from further pain.

Liam stood in the doorway of the sitting room admiring his *mamm's* devotion to her quilting stiches. She had always sewn the most beautiful quilts, and the proof of that was spread among most every *haus* in the community. She was always making a quilt for a birth or a special occasion of some sort, and her unyielding allegiance to the recipient of the gift was a trait he admired most in her.

Emotions welled up in him as he watched his *mamm* from the doorway. How could he strip the smile from her face, when it had only just appeared when she'd brought him home?

Liam cleared his throat as he approached, hoping it would encourage her to acknowledge him before he lost his nerve. He crossed the room when she looked up from her sewing, and sank down in the chair opposite her.

"Steve tells me the quilt shop will be ready for you to go back to at the end of the week."

Nellie set her work aside, her face turned ashen. "You remember everything now don't you?"

Liam wanted to sit at her feet the way he used to when he was a young boy, but he had to be the man he'd grown into and show her he could take responsibility for his actions.

"I remember how much I hurt you and Lydia, and I'm sorry. I acted like a selfish child and I never meant to hurt you. I felt so much shame over *daed's* accident that I didn't think you wanted me around. If I'd gone with him that day, I might have been able to spare this family the pain of losing him. I might have been able to save his life, but I let him go alone because I'd stayed up too late with Lucy the night before and fell asleep in the loft. When he found me, I protested the trip and he allowed me to stay behind. I should have been there with him."

Tears fell from Nellie's eyes, and her expression turned soft. Her heart filled with remorse.

"If you had been there, I would be mourning the loss of my son too."

Liam stood up and ran his hand through his short hair, another reminder of his rebellion. "Isn't that what I've forced upon you all these years? My leaving had to have been just as painful as *Daed's* death for you, especially since I left of my own free will. *Daed* didn't choose to leave you, but I did."

Nellie reached out a comforting hand and placed it on Liam's arm. "If I hadn't been so consumed with my emotions at that time, neither of my *kinner* would have suffered. I couldn't be a parent to either of you then. If I had tried to talk to the two of you instead of letting you fend for yourselves, you might not have left. It's partly my fault that you felt you had no other choice than to leave. I've had to come to terms with that recently, and take a bended knee for abandoning you as your *mamm* during our mourning period."

She stood up and crossed to the window, looking out at the Graber's cornfield that was nearly ready to be harvested. "I let go of my faith during that time. Instead of leaning on *Gott,* I tried to come to terms with the loss on my own. I questioned *Gott's* decision to take your *daed* from us. I was angry and so filled with sorrow that I neglected to see that my own *kinner* suffered the same loss."

Liam stood behind her and placed a hand on her shoulder. "Please forgive me for leaving you when you needed me to step in and take *daed's* place at the head of this *familye.* I should have been brave instead of a coward. I should have stayed and taken care of his *familye* the way he raised me. I let you both down and betrayed *daed's* memory."

"I forgive you for leaving us," Lydia said from the doorway.

Chapter 31

Liam couldn't believe the transformation as he looked at the finished quilt shop. They had moved the last of his *mamm's* things into the building and she would be ready for the grand opening in the morning. He relished the excitement in her as she bustled about the shop straightening and rearranging everything until she was satisfied with its position in her shop.

Her shop.

The Quilter's Square quilt shop had become a reality for his *mamm,* right down to the old sign that she'd insisted on repainting herself. He'd never taken more pride in his work than he had in finishing the shop for his *mamm.* She deserved to have something she enjoyed after all the heartache she'd endured over the years. It was a blessing that had come from the pain of losing her husband.

Liam's crew packed up their tools and loaded up the trucks while he took one final look around. Steve walked out with Liam's *schweschder* giggling beside him. They'd been officially courting for a few weeks, and Liam couldn't be happier for them.

Liam was to meet Lucy next door at the bakery in a few minutes when she closed up her shop, but part of him couldn't pull himself from this moment. This quilt shop had brought him back to his *familye,* and to the woman he'd loved since they were children. But it was *Gott* who deserved the glory for healing their hearts and renewing their love.

Liam stepped over to the display of quilts his *mamm* had fashioned in the front window to draw in customers. Everything looked so professional and pristine; his *mamm* was going to be a huge success with her quilting. Her success as a person far outweighed anything she would achieve among the *Englisch.*

Liam sensed his *mamm's* presence behind him. He turned in time to catch the smile that spread wide across her face.

"*Danki* for this, Liam. Your *daed* would be so proud of the *mann* you turned out to be."

Liam tipped his head down. "But I'm nothing like him."

Merriment permeated Nellie's expression as she looked upon her son with adoration. "You don't need to be a farmer and plow fields to be like your *daed.*"

She placed a hand over his chest. "It's what's in your heart that makes you alike. He was a *mann* of honor, and you have followed in his legacy."

The warmth of her love penetrated his heart. He had found his way back to the life he'd spent so much time running from. Now, it seemed, he couldn't get enough of it.

Lucy put the last of the pastries into a box to take back to the Yoder farm. She'd been spending every evening meal with Liam's *familye* that would soon be hers too. Afterward, Liam would take her for a buggy ride. They had spent many evenings discussing whether or not they would take the classes for the baptism into the church, but neither of them had made up their minds. Lucy had recently told Liam that he couldn't have one foot in both the Amish community and the *Englisch* ways, but she had begun to rethink that statement where it pertained to their future together.

Lucy had to admit that she liked the new Liam—the *Englischer.* She enjoyed taking rides in his truck just as much as she relished the buggy rides they took. Nellie hadn't pushed them into making a decision, and even the Bishop hadn't summoned them for a meeting, though they suspected it was imminent.

If it was left to her decision, they would remain in the community but separate themselves and live more as *Englischers* than Amish, but if she intended to marry Liam, he would have the final say, and she would accept it. She had no desire to wear trousers or learn to drive, but there was something intriguing about watching the *mann* she loved working at his own business, a business built on *Englisch* principles.

Liam's decision to leave the community had given Lucy the courage to openly express her desire to explore the possibility of joining the *Englisch.* She had always been too frightened to consider leaving the community, but with Liam by her side, she felt free to draw from his strength. His love and devotion to her was all she needed, the rest would take care of itself.

Chapter 32

Christmas day, Goshen, Indiana

Lucy sat in the rocking chair of her newly-built home and stared out the window at her husband as he shoveled the porch in preparation for their *familye* to visit. She sipped hot tea and huddled under the wedding ring patterned quilt Liam's *mamm* had so lovingly made for them.

Nearly weightless snowflakes drifted lazily about, while the sun fought to peak through the gray sky. It was still hard for Lucy to believe she and Liam had been married for nearly two full months. Since their engagement, they'd been in a whirlwind of preparations, between the baptismal classes and the baptism, and finally, their wedding.

Lucy looked around the room admiring her husband's handiwork. Their *haus* was the first that

Liam's company had built from start to finish, and Lucy could not be more in awe of his talent as a contractor. She felt overwhelmingly grateful that the community, including her *daed* and *bruder,* had all joined together to help get it built so quickly.

Content with their decision to remain in the community, Lucy was happy especially now that they'd just received the news that she was expecting their first *boppli.* She had never imagined her life could be so full of blessings, when only a few short months ago she'd felt so hopeless. Lucy whispered a prayer of thanks, feeling overjoyed by all that she and Liam had endured.

The front door swung open, snow swirling into the *haus,* as Liam stomped inside. He pulled off his gloves and blew warm breath on his cold hands.

"It smells like Christmas in here. Are you baking my favorite cookies?"

Lucy smiled as he moved over to the fireplace to warm himself. "It wouldn't be Christmas without them."

He shrugged out of his coat, pulling something wrapped in white tissue paper from his pocket. Liam knelt down in front of his wife and unwrapped the paper to reveal a sprig of mistletoe and dangled it above her head.

"It wouldn't be Christmas without a kiss from *mei fraa,* either."

Lucy threw her arms around Liam and pressed her lips to his. It was the happiest she'd ever been, and with the *boppli* on the way, things were only going to get better.

The End of Book 1

THE QUILTER'S SON
Lydia's Heart
Book Two

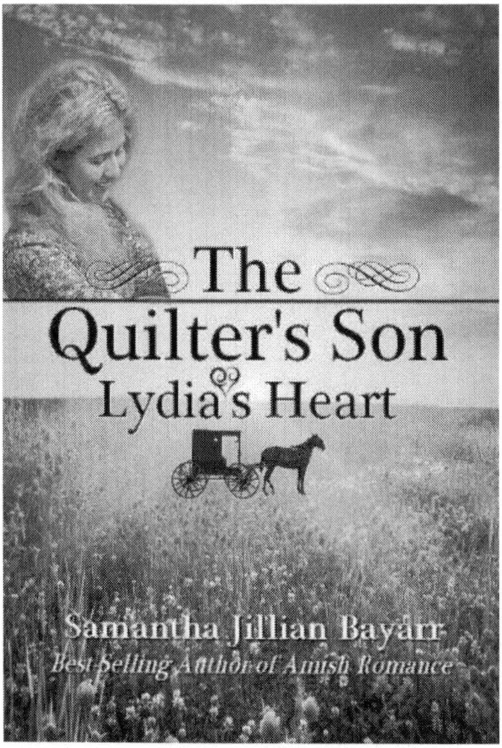

Samantha Jillian Bayarr

All scripture references in this book used from New International Version of the Bible

Chapter 1

"I'm looking for Steven Miller," the woman said. "I need to speak to him regarding his son."

Lydia felt her heart pounding like the force of horse's hooves on a paved road. "What did you say?" she whispered, trying to keep her knees from buckling under her shaky legs. The ground felt as though it would collapse and swallow her. A thousand thoughts ran through her head and she couldn't process any of them at the moment. She tried to keep her composure, but one thought nagged her—Steve had betrayed her.

The older woman, an *Englischer,* stood on the porch holding an armful of folders stuffed with papers, glasses perched on the end of her pointed nose. She lifted open the top folder studying the contents of the first page for a moment. She seemed oblivious to Lydia's shock as she continued to sift through the pages of what seemed to be important documents.

"It has taken our agency nearly three months to track down the correct Steven Miller." she said casually, her mannerism cold and impersonal. "Who knew there were so many Steven Miller's in this area? In the meantime, Nathan has been in the care of a state-run home in South Bend. We are hoping to get him permanently placed with his biological father."

Lydia stared at the young boy, who stood impatiently next to the woman, her vision clouded with denial. He glanced up at her, a strange connection drawing her attention to remain on him. The child, uninterested in what was being said, quickly occupied himself with the iPod he cupped in one hand, and Lydia could hear the music coming from the ear-buds tucked securely in his ears.

Steve had introduced her to the same music over the past year they'd been courting, and she'd discovered she'd liked it very much. Now as she listened to it, the notes suddenly held new meaning as part of the *Englisch* world she didn't belong in.

The child was an exact replica of *her* Steve. His disheveled, sandy brown hair pushed to one side; even the way he stood was the same as Steve. She was momentarily hypnotized by his unmistakable blue eyes that caught in the sunlight and illuminated like the glow of a lantern when the wick is turned up. There was no doubt in her mind that this *buwe* was Steve's *kinner.*

"But Steve doesn't have a son," Lydia heard herself say.

"Miss, where can I find Mr. Miller," the woman said curtly. "I need to speak to *him* about this matter."

Lydia pointed to the back of her *familye* farm. "He lives in the *dawdi haus.*"

The woman and child quickly departed, leaving Lydia to brace herself in the doorway of the main *haus.* How had Steve managed to deceive her all this time? The *kinner* was clearly his. Why had he never even mentioned having a son?

Lydia's mind suddenly switched gears.

Their wedding was in three weeks!

She couldn't possibly marry him now.

He'd lied to her about his past, and obviously his present as well. Where was Nathan's *mamm?* Lydia suddenly envisioned all sorts of scenarios. Was he already married to someone else? Had he visited with his son every time he'd gone to South Bend for a construction job? Most disturbingly of all, Lydia wondered if Steve was still in love with Nathan's *mamm.* He'd obviously not been forthcoming about his past, and she wondered what else he could be hiding.

Lydia closed the door and collapsed onto the nearest chair in the sitting room. Fear constricted her throat, anger gripping her heart with an unbearable force. She tried to stifle the tears that stung the backs of her eyes, but she couldn't. She'd spent the past year courting Steve, taking her time to be certain they were ready to be married. How could she have been so *narrish*—so blind to his deception? Suddenly nothing made sense. The future she'd hoped for became a haze of distorted thought, and Steve was no longer a part of it.

Chapter 2

Steve mindlessly invited the woman and child into the front room of the *dawdi haus,* where he'd been staying ever since Liam had returned home from the hospital. After he and Lucy married a year ago, Liam had moved out, leaving Steve to reside alone in the house that stood just behind the farmhouse of his beloved Lydia.

His focus became faint as his mind processed what unfolded before him.

Unable to take his eyes off the young boy, who'd shyly sat across from him, Steve hadn't heard a word the woman had said to him until one sentence caused his mind to freeze like the water on Goose Pond.

"According to the birth records, Nathan is your son. Since Ms. Foster's death, he's been residing in a group home, but we'd prefer to place him with his biological father."

Steve looked up at her with unseeing eyes; his awareness of the young boy's gaze upon him taunting him.

"Did you have a relationship with Harmony Foster that resulted in the birth of this child?" the woman asked coldly.

How could he answer that question tactfully in front of the child? If Nathan was his son, he would be about seven years old—certainly old enough to understand some of what was being said.

Steve thought back to the night of the senior prom when he'd made that fateful mistake in judgment. He'd been tutoring Harmony in math and had developed a crush on her that he'd mistaken for love. But Harmony was a cheerleader and popular, and would never give him the time of day.

The night of the senior prom, her quarterback boyfriend had dumped her, and she'd turned to Steve for comfort. After, she'd demanded they never speak about what had happened between them and ordered him out of her life forever. Steve never saw her again after that night, and he'd had no idea he'd fathered a child. He'd spent the summer pursuing her, but she'd refused to see him.

At the end of the summer, he received a brief letter from her telling him she was going away to college and that he should forget her and move on with his life. About a year later, he'd received another letter from her, but he'd never bothered to open it. Now, Harmony was gone, and Nathan was inevitably dependent on *him.*

Sweat rolled down the back of his shirt, and he struggled to put two words together. "It was only one night," he barley whispered. "I never saw her again after that. She never even told me she was pregnant!"

"Since you were unaware of the child's existence," the social worker said coldly. "The state will require a DNA test before we can release him to your care."

Steve cleared the lump in his throat. "What about Harmony's parents?"

The woman rifled through a folder on her lap. "According to the investigation, Ms. Foster's mother is deceased, and her father refused to care for the child. If the state can't place him with a relative, he will become a ward of the state and will remain in the foster care system until he reaches the age of eighteen."

Steve looked at Nathan, who was busy playing with his iPod. He didn't need a DNA test to prove the boy was his. He could see it in his haunting blue eyes.

Chapter 3

Steve could see it in Lydia's red, swollen eyes and the way she avoided direct contact with him that she already knew about his past sin—the past he'd kept from her. She'd been crying recently, and he was to blame. She set a plate of food in front of him without even making eye contact. He reached for her hand, but she pulled away.

Looking down at his plate, he noticed she'd made his favorite chicken and dumplings, and had placed an extra biscuit in the corner of the plate just the way he liked it. Why was she being so nice to him when she was clearly upset with him? Guilt hovered over him like storm clouds heavy with icy rain.

He stared at the plate before him as he tried to swallow a bite of the warm biscuit. The food was comforting to him, but her demeanor was unsettling. He could tell she wasn't ready to hear what he had to say just yet, but he said a silent prayer, asking for it to be soon.

Her silence worried him.

They'd never argued or even disagreed before, and if that was what was about to happen, he was prepared to fight for her. He'd never loved another woman, and he couldn't imagine his life without her. The thought of it gnawed at his troubled heart.

Lydia sat across from Steve at the small table in the kitchen, wishing her *mamm* hadn't moved in with her *bruder* and Lucy this week. She planned to stay there until Lucy was back on her feet from having her *boppli.* Though Lydia was happy for Liam and Lucy, the strain of having her *mamm* move in with them created an absence that weighed heavily upon her.

Lydia studied her plate, feeling too distraught to bring the food to her lips, fearing it would gag her nervous stomach. Why had she made his favorite meal? It had been planned at the beginning of her day, and she'd followed through with it as though nothing had changed. But that was not true. Everything had changed the moment she'd laid eyes on little Nathan—Steve's son from an unholy union.

Lydia was tempted to ask Steve the myriad of questions crowding her mind, but she held her tongue. He was practically her husband, and her inherent faith placed him as her authority. Rebellion, however tugged at her faith, warring with her emotions. Anger whispered in her ear, tempting her to believe there was no talking his way out of this, and there was nothing he could say that could take it back.

Her cold heart convinced her there was nothing he could do to reassure her that their wedding would still take place at the end of the month. She wasn't even certain of her own feelings about the wedding. Her faith dictated her duty to forgive, but her sense of betrayal wouldn't allow such thoughts to soften her heart. She felt numb as she sat across from her betrothed, her mind drenched with his betrayal.

Chapter 4

Steve raked at the leaves, the fruit of his labor unclear. The brisk November wind scattered the piles, spreading them across the yard, and brought more down from the trees. If he hadn't needed something to occupy his mind, he wouldn't have even bothered with the task. The sky beheld a definite impatience to bring the first snow of the season, and the chill that permeated his wool coat went unnoticed against the indifference that cloaked his heart.

Pulling down the black felt hat over his ears, Steve pondered the changes he'd gone through over the past year in conforming to the Amish ways. If an *Englischer* were to pass by, they would surely believe he was Amish. He dressed like an Amish-man. He'd even considered taking the baptismal classes and becoming baptized to seal the deal, but Lydia was the first one to decide against joining the community.

Although Liam and Lucy had taken the classes, they had decided not to go through with it at the last minute. Lydia had agreed with them to live as Amish, but to separate themselves from the community. They had already remained pretty separated since their *daed's* death, and there just didn't seem to be any reason to go back at this point. Their decision would prevent them from having to adhere to the rules of the Ordnung, but there was an established community of ex-Amish that they had gotten to know, and they were content with their fellowship with this group.

Now, with less than a month before their wedding, Steve was the most unsure he'd been about his future with Lydia since he'd met her—all because of one mistake he'd made in high school.

Steve thought of young Nathan, who was now alone in the world. He didn't have the heart to deny the boy, even if it meant the end of his relationship with Lydia, and that wasn't an easy reality to swallow. She hadn't spoken more than a few words to him in the past few days, and every time he tried to bring up the subject of Nathan, she'd refused to discuss it.

Today he would be getting the results of the DNA test that he knew without a doubt would be positive. Even though he'd had the past few days to let the reality sink in, he wasn't certain he was ready to face it when it showed up on his doorstep for the second time.

Knowing he'd done all he could to prepare for the boy's arrival, it suddenly occurred to him that Lydia might expect him to move out of the *dawdi haus* and get an apartment in town. He didn't want to leave the Yoder farm, but if Lydia wouldn't forgive him, he couldn't continue to live there. He needed Lydia to understand the circumstances that had brought Nathan into this world. If he couldn't get her to see that he was just as surprised by the child's existence as she was, it would torture him. Still, he was Nathan's father, and he chided himself for not knowing about the child sooner.

It was too late to overthink what he could have done differently when he was younger. He'd not used his best judgment in the situation, and he'd let his emotions make his decision where Harmony was concerned. It saddened him that Harmony was gone, but he'd mourned the loss of her the day after they'd conceived Nathan—the day she'd banned him from her life.

Steve stopped raking the leaves when he heard the car pull up into the lane that led to the farm, but he hesitated in turning around to greet his new son. He needed that final moment before his life was about to permanently change.

Chapter 5

Seeing the results in the context of an official document didn't make Steve feel any more like a father to young Nathan. Shouldn't he feel *something?* He wasn't sure what, but all he could feel was sympathy for the child, and he knew that wasn't the only emotion he should be feeling.

He and Lydia had talked about having *kinner* over the past year that they'd been courting, and the thought of it had always filled him with pride. Now as he stared at Nathan, all he could do was feel sorry for him. Sorry that he'd been without a father his first seven years, and sorry that he was now without a mother.

How could he get past those feelings and learn to be a father to the child when he didn't even feel connected to him in any way? This was not how things were supposed to be. Lydia's face crowded his thoughts, and he wondered how she was going to react when she realized the child was officially his.

Lydia watched through the window as Steve bent down to welcome his son. She rested her aching head against the window, observing the awkward exchange of affection between the two of them. Shuddering against a mournful yawn, she fought the exhaustion trying to overtake her from lack of sleep and being over-emotional the night before. She'd tossed about the majority of the night, dreading the scene that was unfolding in front of her now.

Swallowing the lump in her throat, Lydia fought the urge to run outside, screaming her protest of the whole situation. How could they marry now? Steve already had a *familye,* and she'd not been part of it. The thought of raising another woman's child turned her stomach into knots. It wasn't something she thought she could do. Her thoughts were selfish, she knew, but she'd been dreaming of having a *boppli* with her beloved Steve when they married, and Nathan's presence changed everything.

Chapter 6

"You're asking too much of me, dear *bruder!*" Lydia practically shouted. "I will not watch that *buwe* for him. He's not my responsibility."

"Steve trusts you, Lydia, and you're being selfish!"

She knew Liam was right, but that didn't make her any more eager to do Steve a favor. It certainly wasn't Nathan's fault he was unable to stay on his own, and Steve had thought it was best he not push the child into a new school so soon.

If only her *mamm* wasn't needed to stay with Lucy, then Nathan would be in more capable hands. She couldn't bear the thought of having to care for another woman's *kinner.*

"I need Steve on the job this week since Lucy had the *boppli,* and he can't take his...Nathan with him."

Go ahead and say it, Liam. His *son,"* Lydia said. "Don't walk on eggshells for my sake. My betrothed has a son with another woman, and I'm the one left feeling the shame for it."

Liam pulled her into a hug. "I wish you'd talk to him about this, dear *schweschder.* Steve is having a hard time with this, and he doesn't need you to shut him out right now."

Lydia pulled away from him. "*He's* having a tough time with this?" she practically shouted. "What about how I'm feeling? He's been lying to me since I've known him! I feel so stupid for trusting him."

Liam grabbed her hands and held them to get her attention. "Steve is not the type of *mann* to lie, and you know it. He didn't know about Nathan any more than the rest of us did. I went to school with him, remember? I didn't know about him either. If Steve had known about the child, he would have taken care of him all this time. He would never abandon his own flesh and blood."

Lydia bit her bottom lip to stifle angry tears that burned the backs of her weepy eyes. She knew her *bruder* was right about Steve. He wasn't the sort of *mann* to abandon his responsibilities, but that didn't mean she was ready to talk to him about his betrayal of her trust. He should have told her he'd been with another woman that way. She needed time to sort out her own feelings, and to decide if she could still marry him now that the circumstances had changed.

Looking over Liam's shoulder at Nathan, who stood patiently in the kitchen, Lydia felt a twinge of sympathy for him. It wasn't the child's fault that he'd been thrown into this situation.

"I'll watch him," she relented. "I just don't understand why Steve couldn't ask me himself."

Liam forced a smile. "Most likely because he knew you would react exactly the way you did. I know this isn't easy for either of you, but try not to let your own feelings get in the way of doing what is right. You and Steve need to talk this out and settle it. After all, your wedding is at the end of the month, and beginning your marriage on a note of discord is no way to start your life together."

Liam was right again, and Lydia wasn't happy about it, even though she knew she was being selfish.

She just couldn't help it right now.

Chapter 7

Steve sat across from his dad in the dining room of his childhood home, while his mother placed the dishes filled with pasta and asparagus in the center of the table. The silence in the room was only interrupted by Nathan's constant squirming in his chair. Steve couldn't blame him; he had to keep himself from squirming in his own chair.

Though his parents adored Lydia, they didn't completely understand Steve's devotion to her Amish faith or the community. They constantly questioned why he had to adhere to what they referred to as the "Amish dress code" in order to marry Lydia. He'd been dressing in the Amish clothing since he'd moved to the community, even though he wasn't required to do so since he'd not taken the baptism. He did it out of respect, rather than as a rule the way his parents thought.

Now as he sat at his parent's table, he represented an even bigger weight for them to bear—becoming instant grandparents. They stole glances at the child, who was dressed in *Englisch* clothing, and refused to give up his iPod, despite prompting from Steve to put it away while they ate.

Steve looked and felt out of place in this picture, but he tried not to let it weigh on him. He'd not yet had the heart to transition Nathan to Amish clothing yet, fearing he would only rebel if pushed too soon. It was tough enough that he'd had to give up his school and his friends. He didn't want to push the child into too much change all at once, especially since he'd woken up crying for his mother every night since he'd come to live with Steve.

Eyeing him from across the table, Nathan reluctantly pulled the ear-buds from his ears and switched off the music. He'd charged the battery in the barn for the child since he'd hooked up electricity. Widow Yoder wasn't keen on having electricity come into the house, as she was used to the ways of the Ordnung, but she'd allowed it for the barn to facilitate her son's business once he and Steve had begun to reside there.

Steve knew the music itself was very much in disobedience of Amish ways, but since they weren't part of the Ordnung, he wouldn't push the child into giving it up. If challenged by the new community of ex-Amish that they associated with, he would probably try to argue that the boy wasn't Amish and was too young to commit to the Amish ways. He knew that wouldn't last long as an excuse, especially if Lydia would still have him in marriage. He had seen the disapproving looks she gave him regarding the child's electronic device.

Steve let his thoughts drift to Lydia, who sat quietly next to him. Being too far to take the buggy, they'd taken Steve's truck, but Lydia knew that Steve wasn't comfortable having his parents know that he drove the buggy in the first place. Steve was erratically out of place in Lydia's world, but he hadn't noticed it until just now. She was clearly Amish and he suddenly challenged their *perfect fit*.

Lydia hadn't said more than a few words to him the entire trip to his parent's home, other than to discuss how her day had gone with Nathan. She'd watched the boy for half the day while Steve had finished the porch repair at the Graber farm. It hadn't been much of a discussion since Lydia sadly reported that Nathan sat in the corner reading and listening to his music most of the time. She'd only gotten a response out of him after she offered him warm-from-the-oven cookies and a glass of fresh milk.

Reaching for Lydia's hand during the prayer over the meal, Steve felt the tension in her grasp. He wondered if she would go through with the wedding, or if she would end their relationship over Nathan. He prayed she would forgive him as he clung to her reluctant hand.

Chapter 8

After the meal, Steve excused himself from the table and went upstairs to his childhood room to look for the letter he'd gotten seven years ago from Harmony. It was the reason behind his visit to his parent's home, but he hadn't wanted to say anything to Lydia about it until he'd had the chance to read its contents. He'd thrown the letter in a box and tucked it away in his closet when Harmony had sent it since he was still too bitter to open it at the time. Now as he searched through the box of high school memorabilia, he hoped he wouldn't be filled with regret for never opening her letter. At the time Harmony had sent it, his unforgiving heart was still too broken and unwilling to hear anything the cheerleader had to say. Now he feared it may have contained information about the son he never knew he had.

After sifting through old school papers, he located the worn letter and held it in his trembling hands. He stared at it, knowing that if she'd sent him word of the child, giving him a chance to be a part of Nathan's life, it would be his fault alone that he'd never been able to help raise him. He thought about how different his life would have been had he known about the child. He would have been married to Harmony instead of getting ready to marry Lydia.

Steve opened the letter, fumbling as a photo slipped from the folds of the page. It was a picture of a baby, but he could tell it was Nathan because it looked nearly identical to his own baby picture.

He studied it for a moment.

"It's all my fault," he whispered over the lump in his throat. "If I'd opened this letter, I would have married her and taken care of her and Nathan. Then she wouldn't have had the accident on her way to work. She wouldn't have *had* to work! At the very *least,* I should have paid child support."

Steve stared at the baby picture of Nathan. He'd abandoned his son by not opening Harmony's letter. He had a son who didn't know him, and he was to blame. Guilt tore at his heart, making it difficult to breathe.

He imagined how Harmony must have felt when she'd received no response from her letter. Steve didn't want to think about how much it must have hurt her.

Tears streamed down his cheeks and dripped onto his navy shirt sleeve.

The site of the Amish shirt suddenly angered him. Who was he kidding by dressing like the Amish when he wasn't? What had he been trying to prove for the past year with Lydia? His place had been with his child and the mother of his child. All three of them deserved better than the kind of man he was, and he wouldn't blame Lydia if she changed her mind about marrying him.

Chapter 9

A faint knock brought Steve out of his reverie. Stuffing the still-unread letter into his shirt pocket, he quickly wiped the tears from his face before turning around. Nathan stood in the doorway, and Steve felt the urge to pull the child into his arms and beg his forgiveness. But the relationship was already strained, and Nathan would have no idea the meaning of the guilt that plagued Steve.

"That Lady wants to go home," the boy said casually.

"Lydia?" Steve asked.

Nathan nodded, and then returned his focus onto his iPod. Steve rose from the edge of his bed and placed a hand on Nathan's shoulder, guiding him down the stairs to where an impatient Lydia stood near the front door, her sweater wrapped snugly around her unyielding shoulders.

Steve bid a quiet farewell to his parents who stood by awkwardly waiting for him to take his *family* and leave their home. After putting Nathan in the back of the cab of his truck, Steve stood aside to let Lydia into the passenger side, but she ignored him.

"I thought you wanted to go home, Lydia," Steve said gently. "Why won't you get into the truck?"

She looked up at him, her eyes outlined in pink. He could tell she was about to cry, but he didn't dare reach out to her, fearing she might reject him.

"I don't think I can be Nathan's *mamm,"* she said quietly.

Steve's expression fell. "I don't blame you if you don't want to marry me. I messed everything up for my son and his mother, and now you're agonizing over my mistake in judgment."

Tears pooled in Lydia's eyes. "I *do* want to marry you, but I can't raise another woman's *kinner.* That *buwe* will only serve as a reminder of your betrayal of my trust, and for that reason, I *can't* marry you. It isn't fair to him."

Steve's heart constricted in his chest, and then struck his rib cage with such force he had to cough to catch his breath.

"You want to marry me but you can't? That makes no sense, Lydia."

Lydia crossed over to the large oak tree at the base of the paved driveway, and Steve followed her.

"You lied to me," she said as she turned around to face him. "How many other women have you been with in *that way*?"

Steve knelt at her feet in a desperate attempt to disguise his weak knees that nearly gave out. He looked up at her thoughtfully. "None other than the one night with Nathan's mother. That experience left me with such guilt and shame I wanted to wait for the right woman. *You* are that woman."

Rage filled Lydia's eyes. "You left her after defiling her?"

Steve reached for her hand, but she pulled away from him. "She left me! She ordered me out of her life like a dog! I was young and stupid, and I thought I loved her! I offered to marry her, but she laughed at me. If either of us was defiled, it was me!"

"I'm sorry she treated you that way, but I can only worry about how your *decisions* have affected me. I'm sorry if that seems selfish to you, but I can't help that right now. I wasted seven years of my life being on hold between *mei daed* dying and *mei bruder* leaving me and *mamm*. Now, it seems I've wasted an entire year waiting to marry you, only for everything to be ruined because of your lies and mistakes."

Lydia regretted the words as soon as they left her lips, but there was no taking them back. She'd told him exactly how she was feeling—feelings that had been festering in her wounded heart for the past few days—a wound still too fresh to heal properly.

"I know this looks bad, but it doesn't change how I feel about you. I love you, Lydia, and I pray that you will still marry me. I'll wait on you forever if that's what it takes."

He turned around and walked toward his truck, his words hanging in the air so thick she could almost see them taunting her.

Chapter 10

Lydia sat quietly in the back room of her *mamm's* quilt shop listening to the distorted sound coming from Nathan's ear-buds, while he sat eyeing her from across the room. She made a motion with her hands for him to remove his ear-buds and he complied.

She set aside the quilt squares she was working on. "I could use a break," she said softly. "Would you like some hot cocoa and warm cookies?"

He nodded.

Lydia promptly went next door to where her cousin, Leah, was running Lucy's bake shop while she was out for maternity leave. Lydia was almost grateful for the break from Nathan, rather than from her sewing. She didn't know how to relate to the child that she was still considering raising, and she was still undecided if she would go through with the wedding that was to take place in just a few weeks.

While Leah filled her order, Lydia stared at her reflection in the bakery window. She'd seen the pictures of Harmony that Nathan had brought from home.

She was beautiful.

Lydia, on the other hand, felt very homely in comparison. She knew her true beauty was what came from the inside, and her humble, quiet nature, but she was also aware that Steve had been attracted to a very worldly woman.

Suddenly, her choice of mate seemed more worldly than she'd ever thought of him. Had Steve changed, or had her perception of him changed? Perhaps he'd been the same, worldly person all along, but she'd been blinded by his charm—mesmerized by the allure of his gentle voice. When he spoke, she had a tough time controlling her desire to be in his arms, and that had made it difficult to listen to his explanation of his relationship with Harmony—as if his voice had suddenly changed, and she could no longer tolerate the sound of what was once one of the qualities that caused her to fall in love with him in the first place. Could it be that she would never again be able to listen to that voice she loved so much? He'd promised her a future that he was no longer able to give her.

"I see you brought Steve's *kinner* with you to the shop. Does this mean you're planning on becoming his *mamm?"*

Lydia wasn't ready to answer that question to anyone—least of all to her chattering cousin. Whatever she said to the girl would be spread like fire by the next day to every friend and *familye* member in the community.

Lydia shrugged without answering.

Leah handed her a cardboard drink tray to support the hot cocoa, and a small box filled with warm cookies, and she was on her way back to the quilt shop where Nathan waited for her.

Chapter 11

Awkward silence separated Lydia from Steve as he leaned up against the large oak tree in the side yard that stood between the main *haus* and the *dawdi haus*. She knew Nathan watched them from the window in the front room, and she tried not to let it bother her. Every thought that entered her mind wasn't fit to escape her lips without hurting the *mann* she loved so much it caused her heart to ache. She wasn't certain she was ready to talk to him; she wanted to be left alone to sort it out, but he insisted on taking care of things before too much time had passed.

She was still angry over his betrayal and didn't want to take her anger out on him. As he stood so near to her, it was easier to look off in the distance at the clouds rolling in from the north—clouds that looked like snow. She feared if she looked at him she would break down, and she was not ready to be so vulnerable with him.

She wasn't certain she ever would again.

"Tell me how to fix this, Lydia," Steve finally begged in that sultry tone that made her feel weak in the knees. "I'll do whatever it takes."

"Can you turn back time?"

She hadn't meant for her tone to snap the way it did.

"I wouldn't want to," he barely whispered. "If I did, then Nathan wouldn't be here with me now. If I could turn back time so I could have helped to raise him, then I would, but things have a way of working out the way they're supposed to. I'm sure if I'd have married Harmony, we'd likely be divorced by now. We were never right for one another, but that doesn't change the fact that we had a child together."

She didn't like his answer, but she knew he was right, and she wasn't too happy about that either.

"I belong with you, Lydia." He said, interrupting her thoughts. "That's the only thing I'm certain of anymore. I don't want to do this alone without you. That child doesn't like me, and I have no idea what I'm doing. I've seen you with him. You're good for us. We need you. Please don't make me do this without you by my side. I love you, and can't imagine my life without you."

She almost wished he'd stop talking long enough for her to gather a coherent thought about the situation. His raspy baritone soothed her into submission. It was a sound she wanted to hear every day for the rest of her life. She couldn't imagine going a single day without hearing his voice, but right now it almost set her teeth on edge to listen to him.

He wasn't playing fair.

He knew she couldn't resist his voice or the way he looked at her with those mesmerizing blue eyes of his. He was truly beautiful—inside and out. He was the only *mann* she could ever love, and knowing that gave him the advantage.

"Stop talking for a minute so I can think," she blurted out.

His smirk told her he knew he was getting to her. He didn't have to stand so near as to tempt her to kiss him, but he was enjoying driving her mad with his charm. Steve suddenly closed the space between them and pulled her into his arms unexpectedly. When his lips touched hers it was as if a fire had started in her, the flames so insatiable she couldn't have extinguished them even if she had wanted to.

Chapter 12

Lydia couldn't keep her mind on task as she pieced together the wedding quilt she was making for a customer. It was her third quilt this month, being as it was wedding season among the Amish.

As she pulled the pieces together, she hadn't recalled making the previous ring in the pattern, but she assumed her lapse in memory was due more to reliving the kiss between her and Steve the night before. It nearly took her breath away even now as she thought about it. Her cheeks heated as she recalled the feel of his lips on hers.

Was she losing her mind altogether? Or had that kiss from Steve affected her more than she'd originally thought. It made her angry to think he'd used his charm to try to cover up the sin that was threatening to separate them.

The jingle of the bells on the front door of the shop caused her to rise from her chair, leaving Nathan to himself and his music.

Rhoda Graber stood at the front counter, her eldest daughter, Anna, balancing one of her twin *bruders* on her hip, while Rhonda supported the other toddler in one arm. With three small *kinner* to care for, Lydia could hardly blame Rhoda for commissioning her *schweschder's* wedding quilt with the shop. Lydia couldn't imagine having so much responsibility.

Though Anna was the same age as Nathan, she was clearly far above his maturity level. Had being raised in a Mennonite home caused her to mature beyond her years, or was Nathan's maturity worldly-related? How could she compare the two when they were from two different worlds? She was not unlike Anna, in the same way that Nathan was exactly like Steve. But did those two worlds really merge well without complications? Lydia couldn't help but stare at the girl, and wonder if being in the Amish environment was what was best for Nathan. Lydia reasoned that it was, without a doubt, and his future was in her hands whether she liked it or not.

By the time Lydia returned to her quilt nearly thirty minutes later, she'd learned all about her cousin's mishap on the roof of the Beiler's barn, all the families in the area who had kittens that needed homes, and even about Rhoda's neighbor having her seventh *boppli.* Rhoda could certainly talk, but Lydia had not been in the mood to listen. She prayed she hadn't insulted the woman when she finally ushered her out the door of the quilt shop, but she'd neglected Nathan the entire time.

Lowering herself into her chair, Lydia picked up her sewing where she thought she'd left off, but it wasn't the same. She examined the stitches closely, admiring the technique, but she could not lay claim to it. Her gaze locked onto Nathan, who sat across the room, seemingly not having moved since she'd first left the room.

"Did you…?" she stammered. "*Nee,* you couldn't have."

Nathan yanked the ear-buds from his ears, his eyes tearing up. "My mom taught me how to make quilts," he whispered. "She said it calmed me down when I was too hyper. I'm sorry I touched your quilt without asking, but I was only trying to help. I miss my mom, and sewing the quilt helped me to remember her."

Lydia rushed to his side as he burst into tears. "It's alright. Your stitches are really *gut.* You're welcome to help me, if you'd like."

Lydia's heart nearly broke as she hugged the boy's shuddering shoulders. Perhaps they had more in common than she'd originally thought, for he was the son of a quilter.

Chapter 13

Lydia and Nathan worked side-by-side most of the afternoon, and it was soon time for Steve to arrive to take the two of them home. They'd managed to finish the quilt, and Nathan hadn't listened to his iPod once during that time. Though they'd worked in silence for the most part, Lydia had tried to engage him in casual conversation, but it seemed every subject she broached somehow led back to his absent *mamm.* In her original selfishness toward the child, she hadn't taken into consideration that he was deeply hurt by the void the death of his *mamm* had created.

She knew exactly what he was feeling since she'd lost her *daed.* Fortunately for her, she'd been older than Nathan when she'd had to face the same loss. Still, it wasn't an easy thing to face, no matter how old you are or how much of it you understand, and she'd have to remind herself that Nathan was much too young to understand the full impact his *mamm's* death could have on him.

Death had always been something Lydia feared, and it had only escalated when her own *daed* passed away. She could only imagine that little Nathan must feel like an orphan, and not knowing his *daed* didn't help matters, she was certain. If she, herself, was stronger, she would smooth things between the two of them, but every time she looked at Steve, she couldn't help but imagine him in the embrace of another woman.

The image was almost haunting.

Lydia started packing away the thread and leftover squares of fabric. "*Danki* for helping me, but it's time to put everything away. Your *daed* will be here in a few minutes."

"He's not my dad," Nathan said quietly. "Can't I stay with you?"

Lydia's heart went out to the child, but she didn't want to become a wedge between Steve and his son. Although she alone had the power to fulfill his request, she was still undecided as to whether or not she would go through with marrying Steve.

Her stomach tightened when she heard Steve's truck pull into the alley behind the store. It had made her nervous to be around him the past few days, mostly because she didn't trust herself not to fall into his arms and let him brush aside the tension between them with his gentle kisses. She knew they would eventually have to deal with the subject of Nathan before it festered between them too long, but today was probably not that day; she needed just a little bit more time to adjust to the idea.

When Steve walked through the alley door into the quilt shop, Lydia tensed as she pasted on a smile. She would not let him see how much pain his mistake was causing her, especially not in front of Nathan. It wasn't the child's fault, and she wasn't about to make the situation about *her*. The child had enough to worry about with his relationship with his *daed* without seeing how much his presence had impacted her relationship with Steve as well.

Keeping her composure, she urged Nathan to go to the truck with Steve while she turned out the shop lights and locked up for the day. Instead, the child clung to her side, making things even more awkward for Steve than they already were. She couldn't help but feel sorry for Steve, but at the same time, it warmed her heart to know that the child trusted her the way he did.

Chapter 14

Steve dragged his feet up the steps of Harmony's childhood home. Memories of her father's disapproving looks flashed through his mind as he recalled each time he'd stood on these very steps as a teenager begging to talk to Harmony. Each time, her father had sternly turned him away, saying that Steve's company was not wanted and that he'd caused enough trouble for his daughter. Had the man known back then that Steve was the father of Harmony's child? It was evident, especially after Steve had finally read Harmony's letter pleading with him not to pursue her and Nathan. She'd claimed that her father had sent her away to her grandmother's house and threatened that he would not pay for her college if she didn't abide by his rules for her to put her life back together. She'd claimed it was the only way she could keep little Nathan.

If only he'd known then…

Steve swallowed down his guilt as he knocked lightly on the door. An older man opened the door, but Steve recognized him as Harmony's father. Who could forget those stern eyes? They were much older now and almost appeared very broken. Steve's heart beat fast at the sight of him; it was tough not to feel like a young boy again in the man's presence.

"Mr. Foster," Steve began nervously. "I'm sure you don't remember me, but…"

The older man's eyes narrowed. "Of course I remember you," he barked. "You're the kid who tainted my daughter's reputation, and then left her to raise her mistake on her own."

Steve pushed down the instinct to let his temper flare at the man's accusations. "I didn't leave her! I came over here several times a week the entire summer and begged you to let me see her, but you told me to get off your property! Then when I got her letter telling me she was going away to college, I accepted it was over, but I didn't know she was pregnant, or I wouldn't have given up trying to see her."

"You only wanted one thing from my daughter, and I wasn't going to let you do any more damage than you'd already done."

"You're wrong, Mr. Foster. I would have married her and taken care of her and Nathan."

The old man crossed his arms defensively.

"She didn't need you messing up her life any more than you already did. I took care of her."

Steve's face heated with anger. "By sending her away and keeping my son from me?"

"You did that to yourself," Mr. Foster accused him.

There was no point in trying to argue the past with this man. The past was done and over with, and he couldn't do anything to change it. The only goal he had in mind was to talk about Nathan.

"I came here to talk to you about my son," Steve said cautiously. "He's in the truck."

Mr. Foster waved a finger in Steve's face.

"I told that social worker the same thing I'm going to tell you; I'm not raising my daughter's mistake!"

Steve couldn't believe what he was hearing.

"That's not why I'm here. I want to raise him myself. I just wanted you to know that I won't keep you from being a part of his life."

"I've not been a part of his life thus far thanks to my daughter keeping him from me, so why would I want to see him now? It's too late. The damage is already done, and he doesn't even know me."

Mr. Foster closed the door in his face, but Steve wasn't about to let that be the end of the conversation.

One way or another, he would make sure that Nathan knew he had a grandfather from his mother's side. For now, prayer was the only thing Steve could rely on to fix this.

Chapter 15

Lydia pinned her hair at the base of her neck and stared at her reflection in the bathroom mirror. Since she'd refused the baptism, she'd enjoyed wearing her hair down and the freedom it represented, but it suddenly seemed foreign to her. She was Plain, and there was no getting around that. She wasn't interested in being an *Englischer,* but she no longer fit in with the Amish either. If she married Steve, she would more than likely continue to become more *Englisch* as time passed, until there was nothing left of her *daed's* heritage in her reflection.

Contemplating pinning a *kapp* on her head, she wondered if her *daed* would disapprove of her way of life since he'd passed from this world to the next. She and Liam had changed so much in the past eight years since his passing that she felt her own reflection was nearly unrecognizable.

Had she become an *Englischer* to keep Steve? He'd certainly made some changes for her sake, but it seemed most of the compromise had come from her. What if she married him and raised his child? Wouldn't that also change her? She had to admit that she'd already grown attached to the boy, but she wasn't certain if it was enough to make her want to be his *mamm.*

Grabbing her heavy coat, Lydia mentally prepared herself for the ride into town with Steve and Nathan. She tried to find something to be grateful for in the situation, but up until last week, she'd thought her life was perfect. Now, as she waited for Steve's truck to pull up to her *haus,* she felt it was anything but perfect. Was it Nathan's presence in their lives that had changed things? *Nee,* it was Steve's dishonesty about his past. Her *daed* had always taught her to be truthful because the truth had a way of catching up to you. The truth had certainly caught up to Steve, and it had changed everything for them.

After riding in total silence next to Steve, Lydia rushed out of his truck before he could give her his usual send-off. She didn't want to be kissed by him. She didn't trust herself not to keep her whit about her, and she wouldn't have the strength to push him away.

As she stood at the back door of the quilt shop, Nathan stood at her heels waiting for her to unlock the door. She'd wanted to ask Steve why he hadn't enrolled the boy in school yet, but that would have required carrying on a conversation with him, and she wasn't ready for that either. She was a little annoyed that he was relying on her to care for the child, almost in an expectant sort of manner. Did Steve assume that their wedding would still happen as planned, and that she was ready and willing to accept Nathan as her own child? How could she marry a man she could no longer trust?

She needed to talk to her *mamm.* She worried Liam would take Steve's side since they'd been friends for so many years. He'd already defended Steve, and that irritated Lydia. Perhaps she could work things out over a steeping cup of meadow tea, when she and her *mamm* would have the opportunity to talk freely without interruption or risk of Nathan eavesdropping. Right now, she would push aside her feelings of angst so she could run her *mamm's* quilt shop successfully.

Chapter 16

"Can I help you make the quilt?" Nathan asked timidly.

"*Jah,* of course you can."

Lydia didn't have the heart to say no. Those blue eyes of his reminded her so much of Steve's. How could she love Steve and not have that love trickle down to his son? It just wasn't possible. She couldn't help but feel love for the child. He was innocent in all of this, and he deserved to have a *mamm.* Did she have the strength to raise another woman's child? She'd been asking herself that question repeatedly since she'd found out about him. She was practically raising him now, wasn't she? Steve had left the child with her every day since he'd come to live with him, and to be honest, she'd come to enjoy having him around. That didn't stop her from being annoyed by Steve's dependence on her.

If Lydia made the right choice—the choice she *knew* she must make, then she would officially be Nathan's *mamm.* She knew she was overdue for taking a bended knee and asking *Gott* for the strength to forgive Steve for not being more forthcoming, but she might need a little more time to sort it all out in her head first.

Lydia handed Nathan a needle and thread, and showed him where to begin his neat stitching. She watched his sad eyes come to life as he set to work on the quilt, almost as if he felt connected to his *mamm* in some way. Nathan seemed to be adjusting to his loss better than she'd adjusted to the loss of her *daed*, but given his age, Lydia had to wonder if he was capable of understanding the full impact of the changes that had happened.

"Are you going to be my new mom?" Nathan asked innocently.

Lydia dropped her thimble and bent down to pick it up.

"When my friend, Charlie's, mom died, he got a new mom when his dad got married."

"I have certainly thought about being your mother. Is that alright with you?" She felt awkward discussing this with Nathan, especially without Steve being there, but she couldn't justify ignoring the child's questions.

Lydia looked into Nathan's tired eyes. "I need a new mom, and you're nice to me. I think you would be a good mom for me."

Lydia suppressed the laugh that tickled her heart. She could suddenly see herself as Nathan's *mamm,* but she still couldn't get past the lies of her betrothed. If only she could separate the two, but being the child's mother involved forgiving Steve and going ahead with the wedding as planned.

"*Denki*—thank you," Lydia said.

Nathan giggled. "Will you teach me those funny words you say? And can I get a hat like my dad's?"

Lydia smiled. He wanted to learn her Amish ways, and she was eager to teach him. Perhaps she could be his *mamm* after all.

Chapter 17

Steve was finishing mucking up the stalls in the barn when he heard a scream followed by a thump. Panic seared his heart as his gaze feel upon Nathan where he'd landed on the hard-packed dirt floor of the barn after falling from the hay loft. He'd warned the child not to climb the ladder, but he'd obviously disobeyed.

That didn't matter now.

His son was hurt.

Steve rushed to Nathan's side, the rest of the barn a blur. His focus was on Nathan, as he cradled the crying child in his arms.

"Where does it hurt, Son?"

Nathan pointed to his side. Steve lifted his sweatshirt and could already see the bruising around his ribs.

Lydia rushed into the barn out of breath and ran to Nathan's side. "I heard you all the way from the yard. What happened?"

"He fell from the loft," Steve said over Nathan's crying.

Nathan continued to cry but clung to Steve as he reached a hand out to Lydia. "It hurts!" he cried. "I'm scared."

"I think he might have a few broken ribs," Steve said. "We need to get him to the emergency room."

"Am I going to die like my mom?" Nathan cried.

"You're going to be just fine," Steve soothed his son. "We are going to get you to the hospital, and they will fix you up as good as new."

"You promise?" Nathan begged, gulping at his tears.

"We promise," Lydia said around the lump in her throat. She had to be brave. She couldn't let Nathan see her worry or it might make him even more fearful.

Steve carefully lifted Nathan from the floor of the barn. Lydia walked ahead of him and reclined the passenger seat of the truck so that Steve could set Nathan down without aggravating his injury any further. Once he was strapped in, Steve went to jump in the driver's side.

Lydia nudged him aside and climbed in the back of the cab. "I'm going with you!"

Steve didn't argue with her; he was too nervous to handle this on his own and was grateful she was willing to accompany him in taking care of *his* son.

As Steve tightly gripped the steering wheel, the drive to the hospital seemed endless. He tried to drive as carefully as possible, but every bump in the road caused the child to cry out in pain. Steve apologized repeatedly, but it wasn't enough.

Lydia found herself placing a hand on the child's head, and soothing him with the same words of comfort that her own *mamm* had used on her when she was young. It was all she could do for him, but she could see in his eyes it was welcomed.

Chapter 18

Steve sat down next to Lydia and handed her a cup of coffee from the vending machine in the waiting room of the ER. A nurse walked up to them as Steve sipped the hot beverage.

"Are you Nathan's parents?" she asked.

Steve looked at Lydia awkwardly, and then addressed the nurse. "I'm his dad."

"He's out of x-ray now, Mr. Miller, so you can go in with him." She then turned to Lydia. "You can wait here, Ma'am."

Steve mouthed the words *I'm sorry* to Lydia as he watched her slump back down onto the waiting room chair. His heart was torn as he followed the nurse into the room where his son rested quietly. The look on Lydia's face had been enough to make him cry. He could see in her eyes that she already thought of herself as Nathan's *mamm,* but since they weren't married, she had no rights to the child as far as the hospital was concerned.

Steve sat down in the chair at Nathan's bedside and pulled his tiny hand into his. The child looked up at him with sleepy, red-rimmed eyes. It was obvious they had given him something for the pain, but he was fully aware of his father's presence.

"Where's Lydia?" he asked with a weak voice.

"She has to stay in the waiting room, Nathan," Steve said. "I'm sorry, but those are the hospital rules."

The nurse, who'd been checking Nathan's IV, spoke up. "Only moms and dads are allowed to be in here with you, Nathan."

"But she *is* my mom," Nathan cried. "Go get her and make her come in here with me."

"Okay," the nurse said as she left the room.

Steve looked at Nathan sternly. "Why did you tell the nurse that Lydia is your mom? You know that isn't the truth."

"It *is* the truth," he said innocently. "You are going to marry her, and she will be my new mom."

Steve felt his heart clench in anguish. He prayed that the hope of this innocent child's wish would come to pass.

Chapter 19

Lydia stepped cautiously into Nathan's room, wondering why she had been allowed to visit with him after the nurse had made it painfully clear that she wasn't his parent. It didn't matter what that nurse said; Lydia knew what her heart was telling her. She was ready to accept Nathan as her son and raise him as such. It was time to talk to Steve, and hope it wasn't too late to patch things up between them. Nathan's injury had scared her just as much, she imagined, as if she was his real *mamm*—at least she supposed that's how it felt to be a *mamm*. She loved Nathan, and she loved Steve far too much not to forgive him for his past.

When Nathan spotted Lydia in the doorway of his hospital room, he stretched his hand out to her. She walked toward him without hesitation and closed her fingers over his small hand.

"I told the nurse you were my mom so she would let you come into my room," Nathan said proudly.

Lydia's heart fluttered with pride as she smiled at the boy she hoped would soon be her son.

Nathan held fast to Steve with his other hand. "Dad told me I should tell the truth, but I think God would be okay with me telling what I hope is true."

Lydia was surprised by the child's statement. Not only did he have a working knowledge of *Gott,* but he'd referred to Steve as his *Dad.* It was only the second time he'd said it, but this time, she believed he meant it.

"Did the doctor say when they were going to let you out of here?" Lydia asked.

Nathan shrugged.

"They want to keep him overnight and run a few more tests to be sure he doesn't have any internal injuries," Steve said. "He cracked three of his ribs."

Lydia gasped. "*Ach,* will he be alright?"

"We need to say our prayers," Nathan said.

"I agree," Steve said.

Lydia looked at Steve and couldn't help but smile. She could see by the glint in his blue eyes that he was happy, and for the first time in over a week, she was happy too.

Chapter 20

"I can take you home if you're tired," Steve offered Lydia.

She settled onto the brown leather sofa next to him in the parent's lounge. They were the only ones in the room so Steve had turned off the TV, hoping for a little quiet.

Lydia glanced at the clock, noting the midnight hour. "*Nee,* it's too late now, and if Nathan wakes up and neither of us is here, he might get upset. But if you want me to go home I will," she added, reluctantly.

Steve pulled her hand into his, and this time she didn't pull away from him. "I want you to stay, and I *know* Nathan would want you to stay. He's made it very clear that he wants you to be his mother. I'm sorry if that makes you feel pressured."

"*Nee,* I love the little guy."

"I do too," Steve said. "I didn't think I could, but when I saw him lying helpless on the floor of the barn, I was terrified of losing him."

Lydia shivered lightly in the cold hospital, and pulled a blanket over her. One of the nurses had given them blankets and pillows to make them more comfortable in the parent's lounge in case they wanted to stay for the night. "I have to admit, I was pretty scared myself. It's amazing how much a wee one can take up so much space in your heart."

"I know what you mean," Steve said as he pulled her closer so she could rest her head on his shoulder.

Lydia cuddled up against Steve willingly. She was too tired to fight her desire to be near him. At the moment, her heart was so full of the love she'd thought she'd lost forever that it didn't matter that things were not settled between them. It would seem that the situation with Nathan hadn't broken her heart after all; it had brought it to life.

Chapter 21

Lydia could smell the coffee even before she opened her eyes. Her neck felt stiff from sleeping with her head propped up against the arm of the hospital sofa. She let her eyes drift open slowly to adjust to the bright lights of the waiting room of the pediatric ward. Had she really slept under those bright, florescent lights? She'd never been one to be able to sleep in strange places, unlike Liam, who could sleep during the morning milking if he could get away with it.

Steve sat down next to her and pushed the blankets over her. "Are you ready for coffee? Nathan's been awake for an hour asking for you, but I didn't have the heart to wake you."

Lydia stretched before lifting her aching head. She definitely needed coffee. "I didn't mean to fall asleep." She glanced at the large clock on the opposite wall. It was nearly 6:30am.

Steve nudged her. "I didn't know you snored! If I'd known you snored like that, I might not have asked you to marry me!"

Lydia looked into Steve's smiling eyes and let go of a little giggle. "You were snoring *long* before I ever dozed off!"

Steve chuckled. "I don't snore!"

"Maybe I should be the one to be wary of marrying someone who snores as loudly as you do!"

Steve's expression changed. "Does this mean you're still planning on marrying me?"

She was afraid to answer him right now, but she couldn't let him suffer her silence on the subject. "I want to talk to *Mamm* and sort a few things out before we talk about this. I was planning on talking to her yesterday before Nathan's accident. Will you give me a little more time?"

Steve bent down to kiss her forehead as he handed her a cup of coffee. "You take all the time you need. I don't want you to have any doubts or any regrets. Just know that I'm sorry for not telling you about my past with Harmony."

Lydia let her gaze fall upon his blue eyes that always had a way of looking into her very soul. She could see the remorse there, and she knew he was a man of integrity, even if his past sins didn't support that opinion.

Chapter 22

"Mom, where are you?" Nathan called from the bedroom that Lydia and Steve had set up for him when he'd left the hospital. They both thought he might be more comfortable in the main *haus* since the rooms were bigger with fewer obstacles for him to have to avoid bumping into. He was still sore, and needed help getting up from his bed.

"Mom…"

Lydia was certain she would never get tired of hearing that. She would eventually teach him to say "*mamm"*, but for now, "mom" was close enough to make her heart sing.

"I'm coming," she called as she climbed the stairs for the fourth time since she'd put him to bed. Steve had gone back to the *dawdi haus* over an hour ago, and she was trying to finish the quilt she'd neglected since

Nathan's accident, but luckily, that one wasn't an urgent customer order.

Her cousin, Leah, had been re-routing the quilt shop's customers into the bakery for new orders and pick-ups. In the afternoons, Leah had been dropping off any new orders, along with payment for the three throw quilts she'd finished in the midst of all the chaos. Nathan had insisted on helping her since he was on bed-rest until the end of the week. She was happy for the help, especially since her responsibilities had changed with the new living arrangement her soon-to-be son had requested.

Lydia had quickly settled into a routine with the child, finding it unexpectedly easy to adapt to being a new *mamm.* It wasn't official yet, but she had plans to talk with her own *mamm* tomorrow afternoon over tea. It was a talk she both dreaded and welcomed, although she already knew the decision that rested in her heart.

Chapter 23

"*Gudemariye, Grossmammi,*" Nathan said with such ease, it delighted Lydia.

"*Gudemariye* to you, Nathan," she said as she ruffled his thick hair. "*Wie gehts?*"

"I'm having a *wunderbaar* day quilting with *mei mamm.*"

Lydia's heart skipped a happy beat. It was the first time he'd called her *"mamm"*.

Her *mamm* looked at her and smiled. "I see you've been teaching the wee one quite a lot. Does this mean you've made up your mind, *dochder?*"

"Jah, I've decided to go through with the wedding and become Nathan's *mamm!*" she whispered excitedly as she ushered her *mamm* toward the kitchen.

"You're early. I wasn't expecting you for another hour, so I haven't made any tea yet."

Nellie pulled out a chair and sat down. "I'm a little tired today. If you have *kaffi,* I'd like a cup. Having *grandkinner* is a lot more work than I imagined. It's making me feel old."

Lydia smiled. "*Mamm,* fifty is not old. But I agree with you that *kinner* can certainly wear you out. I'm hoping I'll get used to it."

"When you're fifty, you let me know if you think it's old. Life has taken a lot out of me in the past few years."

Lydia knew she was referring to being a young widow. "*Daed* would have loved being a *grossdaddi.*"

"Jah, he would have little Nathan running this farm by now if he was still with us."

Lydia felt sorry for her *mamm.* She knew how much she missed her *daed,* but she couldn't imagine life without her husband. Life was too precious to throw away the chance to be with the *mann* you love, and that was the biggest reason she decided to marry Steve. She had been miserable since their relationship had been put on hold when Nathan first arrived on her doorstep over two weeks ago.

Lydia watched him from the kitchen for a moment, in awe of the changes in her heart since that day. She had been *narrish* to feel jealousy toward his *mamm,* when she should be grateful to her instead for raising such a *wunderbaar buwe.* She didn't think she could love him anymore than if he was her own *kinner.*

Nellie rested her hand over Lydia's. "You have the glow that only a *mamm* can have."

"I do love that wee one," Lydia admitted. She paused, letting her gaze blur into her future for a moment. "I'm ready to forgive Steve," she finally said.

"What if I come back later so the two of you can take a buggy ride?" Nellie offered. "It will give you the chance to make amends with one another. You don't want to begin your life together only to have it end up in marital discord."

Lydia threw her arms around Nellie.

"*Danki, mamm.*"

Lydia knew she and Steve needed some time alone—something they hadn't had since—well, since they'd stopped communicating.

Chapter 24

Lydia paced the dirt floor of the barn entrance, where she was sheltered from the wind, while she waited for Steve to finish fastening the harnesses on her gelding, Pepper. The horse's speckled flank had earned him the name, and his impatient temperament only added to the designation. Steve had gotten Pepper for her at the auction only three weeks after they'd begun courting, and he'd worked with the gelding faithfully until he was able to pull the buggy.

Stepping outside, Lydia breathed in the crisp November air. Winter would be upon them before long, and she would soon be nestled into her role as *fraa* and *mamm.* She felt a little scatter-brained over the mountain of things she had put on hold for the past two weeks, thinking she would call off the wedding. Now, there was almost too much to do, but she was grateful for her cousins who had offered to step in and help her get everything ready in time. Even though they weren't part of the community, they had a wealth of *familye* and friends ready to support and lend a hand to make certain her day was the most *wunderbaar* day she could ever imagine.

Steve held out his hand to assist her into the open buggy. At his touch, Lydia felt warmth run through her. She settled into the seat of the buggy and allowed Steve to place the lap quilt over her. Lydia felt giddy as he climbed into the buggy and slipped beneath the oversized lap quilt.

She'd missed being so near him.

As Steve picked up the reins, Lydia leaned into him and kissed him on the cheek.

Steve clicked his tongue, setting Pepper into motion. "What was that for?" he asked.

Lydia snuggled in a little closer, resting her head on Steve's shoulder. "For being so patient with me while I worked all of this out."

Steve nodded, not knowing quite how to approach the subject that had put a thorn in her side. They rode in silence for several miles, and Lydia basked in the romance of the ride. Above, the stars seemingly twinkled just for them, and her breath formed bluish clouds against the moonlight. Her mind wandered, the clip-clop of Pepper's hooves lulling her into romantic thoughts about her wedding night.

"I'm sorry that my past mistake hurt you the way it did," Steve gently interrupted her reverie. "You have to know that you are the only woman I have ever loved, or could ever love. I'm sure that sounds terrible given the fact that I have a son, but I was young and did a stupid thing. I hope you can forgive me for keeping my relationship with Harmony from you."

Lydia sighed. "I forgive you, but you can hardly call the relationship a mistake. If not for her, you wouldn't have Nathan. I am very grateful for her, because I get to be *mamm* to that wee one."

Steve turned to her, letting Pepper guide the way down the embankment to Goose Pond. "Does this mean you plan to marry me?"

Lydia paused, making certain she had no doubts.

She had none.

Steve pulled the horse to a halt just short of the willows that encumbered the edge of the pond. He turned to her, his eyes filled with worry.

Lydia smiled at him. *"Jah,* I will marry you!"

Steve's eyes pooled with happy tears. "I love you!"

He tucked his fingers under her chin, lifting just enough so her lips touched his. Their warmth brought encouragement to him after feeling so lost without her the past two weeks.

Lydia leaned into his kiss, making certain he knew she loved him.

Chapter 25

John foster leaned against his mailbox and opened the envelope that had come from Steve. He set his eyes on an invitation to witness Steve marrying Lydia Yoder. Wasn't that an Amish name? He had no idea that Steve had planned on getting married. This woman would become his grandson's new mother

Fear gripped John's heart.

If he didn't show up at that wedding and lay claim to his kin, he might lose the only member of his family he had left. He chided himself for spending so many years being bitter and full of anger. He'd been so hurt he'd felt too damaged to care for young Nathan, and had turned away the social worker when she'd shown up on his doorstep a few weeks past. He'd gotten a glimpse of the child and had seen a hint of his daughter in those eyes, and that had terrified him. How could he let that boy into his heart when he'd lost his wife and daughter already? He'd been too afraid to love again, fearing he'd lose Nathan too.

Thinking back on his decision, wasn't that exactly what he'd done? He'd lost the child simply by turning him away. He'd lost his daughter to a mistake she'd made when she was only eighteen years old. Then, he'd lost his wife to cancer just shortly after sending away his only child, and they hadn't spoken since his wife's funeral, where Harmony had sworn she'd never forgive him.

Attending the funeral of his estranged child had nearly broken him to the point he didn't feel he had anything left to offer her son. Harmony had kept him from seeing Nathan out of spite. She'd never forgiven him for sending her to live with her grandmother when she'd become pregnant.

What he'd thought he had done for her own good at the time had backfired on him and cost him his family. He still believed a broken heart took his wife before the cancer had any chance to do any damage.

It was all his fault.

He'd messed up the lives of his family so terribly he didn't think God would ever forgive him.

John fell to his knees in a rush of emotion. Tears filled his angry eyes, blocking out words of self-destruction. "God, please forgive me for not loving my family the way you commanded me to. I've wasted so much time thinking I was doing the right thing, when I should have asked you for guidance. I've turned my back on my family, and now they're all gone but one. Forgive me for turning my back on you, Lord, and please help me to let go of my stubborn pride and be a grandfather to little Nathan. He deserves to know he has at least one family member left."

Tears fell unchecked from John's eyes, and he made no apologies for them. Thankful he lived on a country back-road where he could speak his peace to God without any onlookers, he snuffed out his tears and picked himself up, determined to do right by Nathan.

Chapter 26

John pulled his truck into the lane of the address on the wedding invitation, startled by the number of Amish buggies parked on the property.

Was he in the right place?

The invitation had been for Steven Miller and Lydia Yoder, but he didn't really think Steve would marry an Amish woman. He thought back to his own wedding, realizing that although he still missed his wife, he felt at peace for the first time since her passing.

He recalled how angry he'd gotten when he'd found out that she had been going to see their grandchild behind his back. Why had he wasted so much time being mad at her when he should have embraced his family for the precious gift they were? He didn't intend to waste another day without letting Nathan know just how much he was wanted and loved.

Nellie prodded across the yard, making certain that all the last-minute things got checked off her to-do list, when she ran smack into a very handsome stranger. He was dressed in a long-sleeved royal blue dress shirt and black trousers. Lose the tie, and place a black felt hat on his head, and he could almost pass for an Amish-man. His striking eyes and dimples almost made Nellie forget her place.

"Forgive me," she said timidly. "I suppose I need to pay attention to where I'm going."

He smiled, taking in her plain attire. He found her to be very beautiful, and it surprised him to think such a thing about a woman he'd never met. "No harm done. Might I trouble you to help me find Steve Miller? I received an invitation to a wedding and I'm not sure if I'm at the right address."

"Steve is marrying *mei dochder,* Lydia."

John cleared his throat. "I see the wedding is about to start, but would it be possible to speak with Steve first? I'd like to talk to him about my grandson, Nathan."

"Kume, he's in the *dawdi haus* getting ready."

John followed Nellie to a smaller house at the back of the property. She knocked lightly and entered at Steve's prompting.

Steve met John's hand and shook it. "I'm so glad to see you could make it to my wedding."

John scanned Steve's clothing, letting his gaze fall upon the black hat that rested on his head.

"Did you become Amish?"

Steve chuckled. "No, but in a way, I have. I'm marrying a wonderful Amish woman."

John cleared his throat. "I came to apologize, and to take you up on your offer to be a part of Nathan's life."

At the mention of his name, Nathan came out of a back room, his clothing matched Steve's.

Steve beckoned the child to his side.

"Nathan, I want to meet your Grandpa Foster."

John bent down and pulled Nathan into a quick hug. "I'm your mom's daddy."

Nathan tipped his head to one side. "She's in Heaven now. I'm getting a new mom today. You will like her."

John smiled at the child's innocent boldness. "I'm sure I will."

He pulled Nathan into another hug, feeling the most alive he'd felt in years.

Chapter 27

Lydia couldn't believe she was about to marry Steve—finally. Unlike most of the women she knew, who were more excited about the wedding than they were about the marriage, Lydia's mind was on the latter. She was certainly more excited about being a wife and mother. Steve and Nathan were nearly all moved into the main *haus,* while her *mamm* had moved all of her things into the *dawdi haus.*

Everything was just as it should be. In just a few short hours, she would be a *fraa* and a *mamm,* and she couldn't be happier.

Her *mamm* entered the room just then. "Are you ready to have Steve as your husband?"

"Jah, I just wish that *Daed* was here."

Nellie placed a hand on Lydia's cheek and smile. "He is. He's in your heart, *dochder.*"

For the time since her husband's death, Nellie felt a peace wash over her…almost as if *Gott* had something else in store for her future.

Lydia glanced at Nathan, who stood proudly next to Steve, her new husband. She couldn't help but feel a swell of pride. She had become a *fraa,* and a *mamm* all in one day, but she was happier than she'd ever imagined she could be. She was married to the *mann* she loved, and because she was now Nathan's *mamm,* he would once again be a *quilter's son.*

THE END of Book 2

THE QUILTER'S SON
Nathan's Apprentice
Book Three

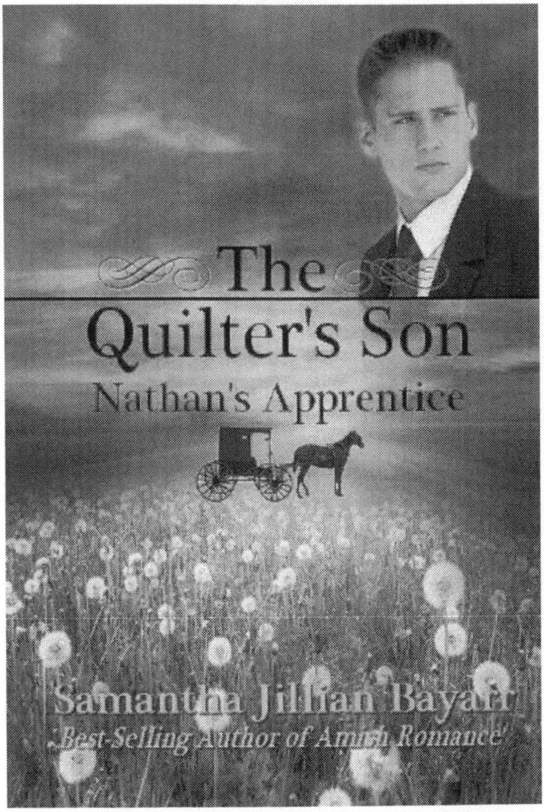

Samantha Jillian Bayarr

All scripture references in this book used from New International Version of the Bible

Chapter 1

"Nathan Miller, you better never do that again, or I will tell your *mamm* just what kind of person you are."

Nathan smacked his lips and wiped his mouth with the back of his hand to make sure everyone in the schoolyard noticed that he'd stolen a kiss from Anna. Nathan had always been the dramatic sort, and getting attention from the others in the schoolyard was one of his favorite pastimes.

"She already knows," Nathan said with a smirk. "She's the one who raised me!"

Stealing that first kiss from Anna in the schoolyard on her thirteenth birthday had set in motion what would later become one of Nathan's favorite things to do.

He loved to get a reaction out of her. She would always pretend to be angry, but Nathan knew she secretly liked it. He'd once overheard her telling her friend, Rachel, how much she loved him and how he better never stop kissing her or she would be sad.

Nathan knew even then, that her resistance to his kisses was all an act. She would always give him that sweet little smile afterword, and the twinkle in her eyes held more than mischief. The two of them were inseparable, and everyone at school knew it.

As they grew older, the kisses became more frequent, And much more meaningful. But there would be nothing that could compare with that first kiss. It would be the first of many kisses shared between them; kisses that with each one would increase in meaning over the years.

Nathan sat on the Greyhound bus headed toward the college campus, recalling the memory as though it had happened just yesterday. That first innocent kiss was just as fresh in his mind as every other kiss between him and Anna over the years. Each kiss had been special in their own right.

Whenever he thought about their future together, that first kiss was always what he thought of. It was his rock, his basis for everything he did to secure their future.

But now, as he sat on the Greyhound bus watching out the window at the corn fields of Northern

Indiana slip by him in fast motion, he wondered if he was making the right decision for both of them.

He had signed up for the special marketing seminars at IU after learning about online businesses while attending the public high school. He was eager to take their quilting business to a higher level; a level that would secure a future where they would never want for anything. With the seminars he planned on attending while at the university, he hoped to gain that knowledge.

Anna had not been on-board with any of it. She'd complained that he had become too *Englisch* since he'd been attending high school. And now, he didn't have the guts to tell her he was considering attending the university in which he was now headed toward.

Lydia and Steve had brought him up to be humble and not want physical possessions, but he had wanted them anyway. He wanted them for his future; he wanted them for his bride, Anna, the one he loved more than anything. He knew that Amish-made quilts were a hot commodity, and he aimed to benefit from his upbringing.

It wasn't until he sat upon his seat on the chartered Greyhound bus, surrounded by his classmates, and watching scenes of rural farm life whirl by his window that he wondered if he was doing the right thing. He should have been honest with Anna about his trip. He should have told her he was also touring the school, and had considered attending the university. He should have told her his student application had been accepted. He'd considered a college education enough to go on the tour, but he knew deep down that he would probably not be attending. If not, he wanted to see what he'd be missing out on.

Again his thoughts turned to Anna and his deception where she was concerned. His intent was to look over the school and get it out of his system so he could go back to his original plan that included Anna and a future with her—a future that didn't include attending Indiana University, no matter how much he might desire it.

And so he let his mind drift to a happier time with Anna, so he wouldn't have to think about the future he would be missing out on by following through with one that he'd already committed to. It was the life he'd wanted with Anna from the very first day he'd met her, and he would not falter. He'd always known he would marry her someday. So why was he suddenly questioning everything?

Chapter 2

Nathan looked over his itinerary for the next five days. He'd managed to cram all the required workshops at the university and a three-day seminar into his schedule during his trip. The seminars were very instrumental to his graduation as well as beneficial to the online business he hoped to create. He needed to pass his business and economics classes at school, and his guidance counselor had suggested the seminars would help him get into college. The counselor had no idea Nathan didn't intend on going to college, especially when he'd agreed to tour the school with the other students that had been accepted. He had gone through with the tour under the guise of attending the seminars needed to set up an online business for the quilt shop.

His only regret now was the argument between him and Anna just before he'd left. Again he allowed his thoughts to drift to his failsafe memory of Anna. Things started off innocently enough between Nathan and Anna, even from that very first kiss in the schoolyard.

It was a gloomy day; not the sort of day that sticks in your memory, but it had made a permanent imprint on his heart. It wasn't so much that day, but more of what the day represented. It was that pivotal point when their friendship turned the corner from innocence to permanence.

If he could've picked a better day for such an event, it would've been a perfect 72°, mostly sunny, with a slight breeze. That to him would've made it more memorable. As it was, he had to fight to hold onto every detail to be sure that not one speck of this memory would slip away from him.

It wasn't that he was against cloudy days per se; it was that he knew that someday when they had grown old and gray, they would talk about that day, and he wanted everything about it to be perfect. It was that important to him.

It was the same day they had started the butterfly quilt, the very first quilt they'd ever made together. It was Anna's idea to make a butterfly quilt. Butterflies were her favorite thing in the world, next to kissing Nathan, as she had later told him.

That first kiss and the butterfly quilt was what set in motion his idea for his entire future with Anna. *That day* was also when he knew he wanted to continue his education at the public school, and it had taken his parents by surprise and caused quite a stir with Anna.

It wasn't that he hadn't enjoyed being raised Amish, it was that his earlier talks with his birth mother about getting a higher education had stuck with him all those years. Lessons about money, responsibility, and securing a better future than what she'd had. It amazed him that her words had always stuck with him, yet he never once remembered her telling him that she loved him. He knew that she loved him in her own way, and it wasn't until he grew older that he realized that he was one of the greatest sources of her stress.

She been a teen mom and had been thrown into adulthood sooner than she was ready. She'd raised him well enough, but still, he hadn't ever been able to shake the words of his birth mother telling him that he needed to make something of himself when he grew up. She wanted nothing short of perfection for his life and for him to be successful both monetarily and personally.

As parents, Lydia and Steve had made sure the personal part of his life was as close to perfect as any life could be, but it was up to him to take care of the monetary part. He wanted to secure a future for him and Anna, the woman he intended to marry.

Chapter 3

Anna sat in her room sulking over the argument she'd had with Nathan just before he'd left for his trip. She'd had a tough time resisting him wearing that *Englisch* suit and tie, but she stood on principle, and she wasn't too keen on the changes he'd described for their lives. What she didn't understand was all of his talk about being successful and making something of himself. It was a little too overwhelming for her to take.

Four long years ago, she had thought that attending the public school was a phase Nathan was going through, and that it would soon wear off. But now that he was about to graduate high school, she'd assumed that would be the end of it—until he'd brought up the seminars last week. All he'd talked about since then was being successful and continuing his education.

If you'd ask Anna, she would say that he was already successful–as a quilter, as a student, and as an all-around good person. She was in total admiration of Nathan and couldn't imagine her life with anyone but him. She'd been smitten with him from the very first time she'd seen him in his mother's quilt shop when he'd first arrived in the community.

That day, she'd stepped away from her mother and watched Nathan sew his mother's quilt with such perfection she couldn't have averted her eyes even if she'd wanted to. She was envious of his stitches that were so unusual and so neat in stature. She knew right then that all she ever wanted to do was imitate those stitches. She was in awe of his natural talent for making quilts and wanted nothing more than to sit beside him while he taught her everything he knew.

It wasn't until they'd begun the butterfly quilt that she realized just how devoted he was to his craft. Over the following years, they'd made at least 500 quilts together, but not one other butterfly quilt. That butterfly quilt had remained in Anna's cedar chest all these years, and she intended for it to go on her marriage-bed.

Now, as she ran her fingers along the stitches of that quilt, it caused her to miss Nathan more than she ever thought she could. Five days would seem like an eternity. They had never spent that much time apart since they'd met, even on his busy days at school.

While the other boys had cut out of school after eighth grade, Nathan had continued his education by going on to the public school with permission from his parents. It'd been something that Anna had supported even though she didn't understand his desire to continue going to school when he had a farm and a quilt shop to take care of.

With Anna’s help, Nathan had taken over the quilt shop since their eighth grade graduation, but with Nathan’s busy school schedule, he wasn’t there as much as she was, with the exception of summers. They could put out a quilt faster than any quilting bee in the community, and it had earned them a lot of business.

Now he talked of fine-tuning those business skills and turning them into an online quilt store. Nathan wanted to take the quilting business to the next level, and his parents had supported his ideas.

Anna wasn’t so sure she did.

Chapter 4

If Nathan could savor the last kiss he'd shared with Anna before they'd said goodbye, it would be what would carry him through the next five days while he toured the campus at Indiana University. He would miss Anna, but he wondered if it was more than opportunity he was missing out on by depriving himself of a college education.

All he could think about was the prospect of going to college on an academic scholarship. His parents would be proud if he'd told them, but he hadn't seen any point since he'd already told himself he would not attend.

If only he knew what exactly it was that he wanted to do about the situation with Anna, then he might be able think a little more clearly.

So here he was, sitting on a Greyhound bus playing tug-of-war with his decisions, when it dawned on him that he didn't *have* to decide now; he could wait and see how things panned out with the tour. If he decided to go, there would be plenty of time to talk to Anna and his parents. He had a pretty good idea of Anna's reaction, and he didn't see it as a favorable one. His dad, on the other hand, would probably insist he accept the scholarship.

Nathan felt a nudge against his shoulder and looked behind him to see Maddie Hayes hanging over the edge of the back of his seat staring down at him.

"Do you mind if I sit with you?"

She didn't wait for Nathan's response. Instead, she pushed by him and sat in the window seat next to him.

Maddie twisted in her seat to face him. "I know this is going to sound dumb, but I know that you like to make quilts and I was wondering if you would teach me."

Nathan was taken aback by the question. He had never invited any of his friends over from school. It wasn't that he was embarrassed of how he lived or his family; it was just that he wasn't sure if he wanted his classmates to know he'd been raised Amish. So for Maddie to know about the quilts he made was a bit of a mystery to him.

He had never dressed in Amish clothing while attending the high school. He did not know why, but he just didn't want anyone at school knowing about his personal home life.

Was it possible that he himself did not really want to be Amish? His dad had never pushed him to live as Amish, though he had adapted to the lifestyle and enjoyed his home life. From what he'd learned, his *mamm* and extended family had separated themselves from the Ordnung before he'd come to live with them, so he didn't know much about it. All he knew was farm-life mixed with his own desire to be more *Englisch* than Amish.

He never really thought about it too seriously until now, but he guessed that deep down he was avoiding being Amish. He really loved Lydia, his *mamm,* and he had always thought of her as his true mother. But when it came right down to it, he had to admit he was a little uneasy about the idea of the public school kids knowing about her heritage. He knew how cruel others could be if they find out you're different, and he didn't want to be teased.

He looked at the impatient girl beside him, momentarily forgetting that she'd asked him a question. He didn't understanding why she was asking him about quilting or how she knew about it, but he didn't really see any harm in teaching her how to quilt.

"Yeah, sure, I can teach you."

"I heard you made a really nice butterfly quilt when you were younger. I really like butterflies and I'd like to make one of those too," she said with a smile.

Nathan clenched his jaw, wondering how she knew about the quilt. "That butterfly quilt was a one-time thing," he said. "There won't be another one like it being made by me."

Maddie leaned into him smiling and fluttering her eyes. "Won't you please help me make one? You don't have to make it yourself, just show me how to do it."

“It isn’t that easy,” he said, trying not to show how nervous he was to talk to her about this.

Maddie shook her head. “I overheard you telling the guidance counselor that you could sew a quilt on your own in only a few days.”

That’s how she knows!

Nathan shrugged. "I suppose there isn’t any harm in showing you how to do it yourself."

Maddie moved her arm on the inside of Nathan's arm and smiled brightly. "Then it's settled. After the required workshops tomorrow we will go shopping for material and you can start teaching me at once so it will be finished by the time we have to return home."

Nathan wasn't so sure about going shopping with Maddie, but the idea of shopping for fabric in a large outlet in the city obviously intrigued him. He didn’t think Anna would approve if she knew about it, but he didn’t have to tell her if it was only going to upset her. He didn’t like adding to his already deceptive trip, but he couldn't resist the chance to show off his quilting skills to the prettiest cheerleader at his school.

Chapter 5

Nathan wondered if Maddie was intending to sit with him the remainder of the trip, but he didn't ask her. Instead, he pulled out his iPhone and sent a quick text message Anna. He'd gotten her a cell phone recently, stating that she needed it if she wanted to work with him at the quilt shop.

Mostly they didn't use the cell phones for anything other than texting each other. Right now he missed her more than anything, and all he wanted to do was smooth things over and mend the fight between them.

If he couldn't settle things between them, it would be a distraction for the next week while he juggled campus tours, workshops, and marketing seminars, and he didn't need that right now. He was on his way to college—even if it *was* only for the next five days.

As the farm scenery faded, so did Nathan's ties to his family. His dad had offered to drive him to the university, but he was too independent for that. He'd wanted to show his independence and ride on the bus with his classmates. Now he wished he had taken his dad up on his offer, for he was the loneliest he'd felt since his birth mother had died when he was younger.

Nathan opened his eyes slowly as the bus came to a halt. He hadn't realized he'd dozed off on the last leg of the trip from Indianapolis to Bloomington. He'd been so anxious the night before that he hadn't gotten much sleep, and he wasn't surprised at dozing off on the way there. He was much like his Uncle Liam who could fall asleep anywhere anytime without a problem. Luckily, Maddie was no longer sitting beside him.

The moment Nathan stepped off the bus onto the campus, the place he would call *home* until Friday, he felt instantly in his element. He worried that Anna hadn't returned his text messages, but he tried to push it aside so he could enjoy his first taste of college life. Nathan knew that Anna would eventually forgive him, but he'd left after they argued, and she'd begged him to stay. His refusal to stay had hurt her, he knew, but he still stood by his decision that this was what was best for the two of them.

What Nathan feared most was that the week would go by so slowly that it would give Anna too much time to stay angry at him. His heart already ached for Anna, and he could only imagine how she was feeling after he'd refused to stay. The look on her face as he'd left for the bus station would be etched in his memory far beyond the course of his trip. He would have to try to find a way to make amends until he could see her again.

Nathan's continued education through the public school had always been a source of animosity between him and Anna, as if she hadn't taken him seriously until he followed through with it. She had made a few remarks about his education making her feel dumb around him, and she'd worried that it would be what separated them—much the same way it was now.

His birth mother had always made sure he had everything that he needed, except the one thing he had not gotten until Lydia began to raise him. Lydia, his *mamm*, had raised him with the love and support of a nurturing family, and that had given him the confidence he needed to continue his education.

His dad, whom he hadn't met until he was seven years old, had also been one of the best things that could have ever happened to his life. His parents had both been very supportive, but Anna, he suddenly realized, had not.

Chapter 6

Being on a real college campus intrigued Nathan. It filled him with an insatiable hunger for a higher education than he'd already received. He'd always thought of college as unattainable, given his family situation, but here he was faced with the biggest possibility to make his dreams come true. His secret dream had been to go to college and get a degree, but his lifestyle didn't support the need for such a thing, and that saddened him. In his present situation, he had no reason to justify the need for college. He was raised Amish and was planning on marrying a Mennonite woman, so the highest he could justify his education would be what he was about to finish in the next few weeks at the high school, nothing more.

As Nathan stood beside the bus waiting for his bag to be removed from the undercarriage, he studied his map of the campus. All around him happy couples held hands. There were no sad goodbyes here like the one he'd had a few hours ago with Anna. The kiss between them had been bittersweet, almost as if it would be their last. It was more than he'd expected from her since he knew she was angry with him. He wished he could share this with her, but the two of them suddenly seemed worlds apart.

Nathan pushed thoughts of Anna and home out of his mind. He was excited that he was touring the campus and checking out the school he'd been accepted to attend, but it upset him more than he realized that he knew he would *not* be attending in the fall.

He had not told his family or even Anna that he'd been accepted to the school, only that he was attending this week's seminars about marketing and business. He had used the seminars as an excuse to come on the trip. None of his classmates were attending the seminars, only him.

Using the map, he walked with the rest of his classmates over to the student housing buildings.

Nathan used the key to open the dorm room where he would be staying for the next five days. The dorms were offered as an incentive to sign up for student housing, but Nathan hadn't spent time alone since he'd been with his birth mother and couldn't really remember what it was like. His much younger siblings had not afforded him much privacy or time to be alone over the years, and there had been times when he'd longed to be an only child again.

Indiana University had been Nathan's goal for a few years now, but he knew it was out of his reach. It didn't matter that he'd been accepted into the business program thanks to his business and economics classes that he done so well in during his last two years of high school.

Nathan entered the small bathroom to wash his face brush his teeth. Then he put away his belongings in the small bureau provided for him. It was still early, but they were expected to attend their first workshop in the auditorium at two o'clock. He wondered if he had enough time to check out Woodburn Hall, the business and economics center, before he was supposed to meet everyone for the financial aid workshop.

Being a business student had been his dream for some time. Unfortunately, the decision rested on the fact that he was the son of a construction worker/farmer and the son of a quilter, and that's what he expected to be for the rest of his life.

His parents didn't have the money to send him to school, and financial aid would not cover all his expenses. He had discussed the situation in great length with his high school guidance counselor, and she'd suggested student loans to supplement his education expenses. Unfortunately, borrowing money was not something the Amish did. And though he wasn't Amish by blood, he was by association, and for that, he wouldn't even consider it as an option.

He didn't mind being the son of a quilter since his birth mother and grandmother had been the ones to teach him to quilt, but he had no intention of becoming a farmer had no interest in building houses with his dad and Uncle Liam.

He wasn't handy like his dad; he was clumsy, and feared falling from rooftops. His smarts and ideas were what made him who he was, and education made him feel less clumsy.

Knowing he had very little time before he was supposed to meet his classmates for the first real tour of the campus with a workshop to follow, he hurried down the steps of the student housing, checking his map to be sure he was heading toward Woodburn Hall.

As Nathan stepped out onto the sidewalk headed toward Woodburn Hall, Maddie rushed up behind him and tapped him on the arm.

"Where are you headed off to so quickly?"

"I'm just looking around a little bit. I wanted to take a little tour on my own before the actual tour started."

Maddie linked her arm in his and matched his walking pace.

Was Maddie going to be his permanent shadow this entire trip? He tried gently to pull his arm away from hers, but she had quite a hold onto his arm. He didn’t want to be rude or make a scene, but he didn’t like her forward behavior. He supposed it was just her way, but he didn't want her to misunderstand his position. He was betrothed, even if Maddie wasn't aware of it.

Chapter 7

The sunny day helped to bring Anna out of the clouds in which she'd been feeling ever since Nathan had left. It had only been half a day that he'd been gone, but it had already seemed like an eternity. How would she ever get through five whole days without him? She didn't want to be another minute without him, for her heart had begun to break and felt empty within the first five *minutes*. If being bored and unhappy was what she could expect to feel until Nathan's return on Friday, then she wanted no part of it.

Before he'd left, Nathan had promised her that they wouldn't want for anything when he returned, but she had no idea what she was signing up for when she'd reluctantly agreed to his plan. While all of her friends were busy planning their weddings, Anna's life was seemingly on hold until Nathan could make his life a success.

It made her angry that she had to wait for her life to begin until after Nathan fulfilled his dream of a higher education by graduating from high school. But now he'd put another condition upon their future, and that involved him turning the quilt shop into an online business. She didn't want the *Englisch* ways to invade their lives, but Nathan was determined.

Even though his graduation was just around the corner, it seemed like she had waited forever for that day to arrive. She almost felt stupid and inferior around him since she hadn't gone past the eighth grade. She didn't begrudge Nathan his dreams, but at the point where they affected her dreams for her future, she wasn't sure she had the strength to bear it. If she protested his plan in any way, she feared that she stood the chance of losing him forever to the outside *Englisch* world of which she wanted no part.

Though he was fully *Englisch*, his Amish upbringing had had no bearing on his plans for the future. He was still undecided if he intended to live among the Amish once he graduated. Anna, being Mennonite, fully intended to remain in the community amongst the cousins and family where she felt safe and secure. In the back of her mind she worried Nathan would never return from his trip, but that was the chance she took in trusting him that his plan was what was best for both of them.

Chapter 8

Nathan wondered if Maddie was forward all the time, or if it was just his suit causing her to cling so closely. Anna had warned him it had had the same effect on her. Maddie had never paid him any mind before, so why now? If she was going to hang around him the entire time and be his shadow for the next five days, it was going to be tough to keep his concentration. He was here for a reason, and that was to soak up all he could about the campus so he could get it out of his system and go back to Anna as planned. With Maddie hanging around, he feared she would pick up on the true reason for his trip. He suddenly wished he hadn't agreed to teach her how to quilt.

Nathan didn't need Maddie as a distraction right now. He had things that he had to do while he was here, and that did not include making a quilt with Maddie. Unfortunately for him, he was not the type who could just blurt out his concerns and tell her to go away. Nathan was well aware of who she was: the popular cheerleader who was in all the clubs and loved by everyone. He hadn't thought she even knew he existed. It had bothered him ever since she'd asked him to teach her, and he wondered how she knew about the butterfly quilt.

Looking at her, he decided he should just come right out and ask her.

"How did you know about the butterfly quilt?" he asked.

Maddie stopped walking and turned to him and smiled. "One day I was walking through downtown and I saw this Amish boy who looked just like *you.* He walked into a quilt shop, so I followed him. When I looked through the window of the shop and saw *him* take off that straw hat, I knew it was *you.* I saw you talking to that pretty Amish girl and I knew I had to find out exactly what you were all about. So the next day, I ditched school, and went into the quilt shop, and had quite a long talk with Anna, your girlfriend."

"She isn't my girlfriend. She is my betrothed."

"Your betrothed? That is quite the old-fashioned word, don't you think, Amish Boy?"

Nathan yanked his arm out from around hers. "Don't call me Amish Boy."

Maddie smiled wryly. "That's what you are, Amish Boy." She turned her lip into a mock frown. "I'm guessing you don't want anyone at school to know your little secret. Otherwise you wouldn't be dressed in a suit today. I've never seen you wear that Amish get-up to school, so you must be trying to hide it. But why?"

Nathan turned and walked away from her, but called over his shoulder. "I don't owe you or anyone else an explanation."

Maddie ran after him. "Wait a minute. I really want to know why you're hiding this from everyone at school. Surely you don't want everyone to know, and there's a reason for that. Maybe we can help each other out."

Nathan whipped this head around to look at her. "How can *you* help me?"

Maddie smiled again, and this time it wasn't a sweet smile. "You help me with my quilt, my *butterfly* quilt, and I will keep your little secret for you."

Anger rose up in him. "Are you blackmailing me?"

Maddie giggled nervously. "I didn't know an Amish boy would know what the word *blackmail* means."

"You think I'm stupid because I was brought up Amish? I got accepted into this college just like you did; only I got in on an academic scholarship. How did *you* get here? Cheerleading? It seems to me that it doesn't take a whole lot of brains to be a cheerleader, but I'm here for a serious reason. My only goal is to check out the college, and that doesn't include spending time being blackmailed by you. Just because I was brought up Amish does not make me uneducated."

He knew he was being rude to her, but part of him felt a little exhilarated for giving her nastiness right back to her.

“From what I hear, the Amish are pretty ignorant and backward."

"Only an ignorant person would make such a comment. If you knew anything about the Amish, you wouldn't make a remark like that. They are the most gentle and humble people I know. Leave me alone."

Maddie grabbed his arm. “Before you go, do we have a deal?"

Nathan gritted his teeth, not enjoying being blackmailed, but he had no other choice. He was not ready for his classmates to find out his secret. He wasn't ashamed, but he wasn't so sure he was convinced of that himself.

"We have a deal. And that's all it is—nothing more."

Maddie chuckled knowing that she had won this round.

Chapter 9

Maddie tucked herself into the chair beside Nathan in the auditorium and nudged him with her elbow. "Where's your suspenders Amish Boy?"

Nathan slighted his eyes to the left and to the right, making sure that no one had heard her comment. His heart pounded with anger and worry, and he didn't like the position she was putting him in. "I thought I told you to leave me alone."

"And I thought we had a deal. As soon as this assembly is over, you and I have some shopping to do."

Suddenly, the thrill of shopping at a fabric outlet had lost its appeal to Nathan.

"I said I would teach you how to quilt and that doesn't mean that you have to be my shadow this entire trip. I am here for a reason, and I have seminars to go to this afternoon."

"Then we can go after your seminar," Maddie insisted.

"It will be too late by then," Nathan snapped.

Maddie smiled. "Indianapolis is nothing like Goshen. The city doesn't shut down every night it dusk. We can take a taxi into the city and go to the outlets."

"I'm already exhausted from the bus trip here, and I have a full schedule ahead of me for the next several hours. I'm not going to feel much like going shopping today if you don't mind."

"Oh but I do mind. And if you don't go with me, I'll tell everyone right here and now you're an Amish boy."

Nathan had no idea Maddie could be so cruel. But he'd heard similar things about the cheerleaders and how mean they were to others. Now he was experiencing that first hand.

Nathan felt defeated and bullied.

"I'll see how I feel when I get out of my seminar."

Nathan stood up and moved over a row of seats to get away from Maddie. He was here to learn about the school and to concentrate on the decision that lay before him, and he had no room for distractions. Maddie stood up and moved toward him and he knew he was in for a long week of this. Was she really going to sit with him during every assembly?

Nathan tried his best to ignore her as he listened to the instructor at the front of the auditorium. There were at least one hundred other students in the auditorium from schools in other counties. He felt lucky to be among them, but Maddie's presence was enough to set his teeth on edge.

After a brief slideshow, the students were asked to assemble outside the auditorium to prepare for the campus tour. Maddie slipped her arm in his once again, making it difficult to concentrate on the tour and enjoy the many points of interest on the campus.

They toured the student center with its Olympic-sized swimming pool and indoor running track. In the center of the fine arts Plaza was the Showalter fountain. It was a warm day, and Nathan couldn't help but think about how many students had probably taken a dip in the fountain. According to their tour guide, students had put a dozen carp in the fountain pool as a prank in the 1970s.

Temporarily mesmerized by the brass fish sculptures surrounding Venus in the fountain, spurting crystal clear water from their mouths, and the coins that glistened at the bottom of the pool, he thought about Anna and wished he could share all of this with her. He was certain Anna would not approve of Maddie being so clingy toward him. There would be no explanation for it, especially since he would never tell Anna that Maddie was blackmailing him.

Anna had asked him on a few occasions if the reason he dressed in *Englisch* clothing when he attended the public school was because he was embarrassed of his Amish upbringing, and he had always denied it.

This was not something he felt comfortable sharing with her, no matter how close they were. How could he explain to Anna that part of him really was embarrassed, especially since he couldn't even explain it to himself?

Chapter 10

Inside the vast, Lilly Library, which was dedicated in 1960, Nathan learned that it contained close to a half a million books. He looked around him in awe, wondering if a person could ever read that many books in a lifetime. He chuckled at the thought of trying to read that many. He had never seen so many books in his entire life, and he couldn't imagine how many books there must be in the world. It seemed as if there was a lot that he was missing out on because of being in the Amish community, but there was also something to be said about the humbleness of community life and having those around you who love you.

When the tour had come full-circle and they had returned to the auditorium, Nathan's attention was drawn toward the tops of the high walls where painted murals depicted the social progress of Indiana. According to the tour guide, those same murals were exhibited in the 1933 Chicago World's Fair. Nathan was in awe of such talent and couldn't imagine painting such massive works of art.

At the conclusion of the financial aid workshop, Nathan stood and started to walk outside with Maddie on his heels.

"Are you going to your seminar now?"

"Yes I am. And I have to find this classroom a few buildings over before I'm late."

Maddie looked over his shoulder and studied the map with him, looking for the direction of the building in which he needed to go.

"Can I go with you?"

"No you can't go with me. You didn't sign up for it."

"Is it free?" she asked.

"Yes it's free." He said, annoyance evident in his tone.

Maddie smiled, and hooked her arm in his. "Then I can go with you."

"No you can't go with me," Nathan said, trying to peel her arm away from his.

He was getting more annoyed with her by the minute and regretted giving in to her earlier demands. He had shown weakness from the start, and now she knew she could push him around.

"Why are you even attending the seminars? What are they for?"

Nathan tried hard not to be short with her, but she wasn’t making it easy for him to be kind. He had been taught to be of a quiet spirit and kind to everyone no matter what the situation, but she was trying his patience.

"If you must know, I'm attending the seminars to learn marketing skills to take my quilting business online."

"I thought the Amish didn't use computers. Is your Amish girlfriend okay with you taking your business online?"

Nathan looked off in the distance to avoid eye contact with her. He was certain that if he looked directly at her during the conversation he was going to yell at her. The surrounding grounds helped somewhat to calm him as he walked through the campus toward his destination.

"Anna isn't Amish, she's Mennonite. And she isn't my girlfriend, I am engaged to be married to her."

Maddie scoffed. "Why would you get engaged in high school? That is so stupid on so many levels. I can’t even begin to tell you how that would ruin your future."

Nathan sighed, feeling unnerved by her constant questions and ridicule. "We aren't actually engaged yet, we are promised to each other to get married as soon as I graduate."

"Is that really what the Amish do? They get married so young that they don't even take the time to have a life?"

Nathan shot her a look of disgust. "Anna *is* my life, and so is the Amish community and my family."

Maddie scrunched up her face in confusion. "Then why are you here? Oh, wait a minute. You don't really intend to go to college here, do you? You are only here to go to the seminars. The Amish don't allow you to go to college, do they?"

Nathan was growing weary of her questions. "We aren't actually part of the community, since my mother left the Ordnung."

Maddie smiled. “Does that mean you can date and marry whoever you want to?"

Nathan pursed his lips. "I intend to marry Anna. I *want* to marry Anna."

"If you ask me, I think you're here because maybe you really don't want to marry your precious Anna."

Nathan increased his pace, intending to walk away from her. He was not going to put up with another one of her accusations, even if there was *some* truth to it.

Chapter 11

Nathan sat beside Maddie in the taxi as they rode through the busy city looking for the fabric outlet she found through a Google search. Nathan was more worried about how much the cab fare was going to cost him than finding the fabric outlet at this point. They had gone quite a distance from Bloomington searching for a fabric outlet off interstate 70.

When the taxi finally pulled up to a large strip of buildings resembling an outdoor mall, Nathan reached into his pocket to retrieve what he hoped would be enough cash that he'd set aside for the cab fare.

Maddie pushed his hand aside, telling him she had it covered and not to worry. He was all too happy to let her pay the fare since this trip was her idea in the first place.

As they stepped into the store, Nathan was in awe of the selection of fabrics and all the things they didn't have in the fabric store in Elkhart. Nathan wandered around the store while Maddie picked out several shades of pastels to make a quilt. Nathan helped her calculate the correct yardage needed for the size of quilt she wanted and then left her to decide which ones she would mix together for the pattern.

Nathan found himself lost in the thrill of the possibilities for making future quilts from the variety of fabric styles. Quilts were his life. It was what he knew. Nothing made him feel more inside his element than to run his fingers over a nice piece of fabric, imagining the possibilities and seeing the finished product in his mind's eye. Quilting was who he was. He was a quilter's son. He had always hoped someday that he would have a son that he could pass on his knowledge to that would follow in his footsteps.

Nathan thought of Anna and how much she would enjoy seeing this place. He could just imagine the look on her face at all the selection of different fabrics styles and textures. Reaching into his pocket, he counted the money that he had. He'd saved aside enough for expenses on the trip but found there were none since their meals and shelter had been provided for by the university.

He'd even tucked away some "just in case" money, hoping to find something that he could get for Anna since he knew he was going into the city. Fingering a particular yellow calico that he knew would delight her, he decided to buy enough to make a new quilt.

Seeing that the fabric was on sale, Nathan decided to get it in blue and pink as well. He knew Anna would be so happy to have the fabric in a pattern that they were unable get in Elkhart. It would make a nice quilt; one that they could keep for themselves or they could put in the shop for display. Knowing that he could mix and match all three fabrics to make three different quilts, he was delighted with his choice. And he knew Anna would be happy too.

Maddie came up from behind him and startled him from his reverie. "Are you buying that for your quilt shop?" Maddie asked.

Nathan nodded, not feeling considerate enough to formally answer her. He was over this trip and eager to go back to the dorms so he could do a little bit of research regarding the things he'd learned during his first seminar.

"I'm hungry," Maddie complained. "Can we go get some dinner at the restaurant around the corner?"

Nathan shook his head. "Not only is that not in my budget, I'd like to get back to the dorm rooms so I can do a little bit of research."

Maddie tipped her head to one side and fluttered her eyelashes at him. "It will be my treat. Please?" She begged.

The last thing Nathan needed was for her to ridicule him and make some snide remark about him being Amish and poor. So he accepted her invitation even though it went against his better judgment.

Chapter 12

Nathan tossed and turned in the unfamiliar bed, unable to sleep. It wasn't so much that it was a strange bed, but that he had a guilty conscience. He felt guilt over having dinner with Maddie, especially since he'd actually had a good time. For one full hour, he'd forgotten all about Anna.

Now, realizing he'd never taken Anna out to dinner at such a nice restaurant, he felt more guilt than he could handle. It gnawed at him, nearly to the point of making him feel ill. If Anna knew what he'd been up to since he'd left her side, she would be ashamed and disappointed in him.

He would be lucky if she would forgive him and take him back after the careless way he'd been acting. It had all started with that one lie, that lie about being accepted at the University. And now he'd added another lie—in having no intention of telling Anna the truth about his dealings with Maddie. The stress was more than Nathan could stomach.

There was no way he could get Maddie off his back fast enough. If he could get through this week and get her well on her way to making the quilt that she so desired, then he could get away from her and would never have to have anything to do with her ever again. The only dilemma then would be whether or not to tell Anna everything.

After twenty more minutes of tossing and turning, Nathan decided it was best if he helped Maddie, hoping never to see her again. He would keep it to himself never to speak of it again. It wasn't a great plan, but it was his only plan.

Chapter 13

Nathan yawned and stretched as he fidgeted in his chair in the auditorium, trying to concentrate on the lecture about school policy. All he could think about was Anna, but that was difficult to do with Maddie cozied up beside him. She was relentless, unyielding in her quest to pursue his help in making the quilt. How would he ever get through this week? It was going to be pure torture. How was he even going to get through this lecture with Maddie’s closeness weighing on his mind? It wasn't that the lecture mattered, especially since he didn't plan on attending the university. He was wasting his time here he knew, but he was expected to sit there and be in attendance in order to afford him the avenue to attend the seminars.

If this lecture wasn't required, he would jump from his seat like he wanted to and get away from Maddie as quickly as possible.

Unfortunately, he had to remain in his seat and at least pretend to be paying attention for the sake of his trip. He was beginning to wonder if any of this was worth what he was putting himself through, especially with what Maddie was currently putting him through. Feeling Maddie's head drop against his shoulder suddenly, Nathan felt like he wanted to jump out of his skin.

Instead, he jumped from his chair abruptly catching the attention of the lecturer. Nathan could've made an excuse for himself such as needing to use the restroom, but he was an adult now and didn't feel the need to give an explanation. He nearly ran from the auditorium as quickly as possible and headed back to his dorm room.

Nathan fumbled with the key trying to open the dorm room door.

"Since you don't have any intention of staying in the lecture," Maddie said. "Perhaps we could get busy on that butterfly quilt now?"

Nathan could feel emotion clouding his thought process. "I'm probably going to get kicked out of here now that I left the required lecture, and all you can think about is making a quilt?"

Maddie laughed heartily. "This is college; they don't kick you out for missing classes. Why would they kick you out for missing a lecture on student policy? You're old enough to read the handbook, and they know that. You *can* read, can't you, Amish Boy?"

Nathan felt anger course through his veins at her accusations. He was trapped in a lie he helped to create, and there was only one way out of this mess.

Chapter 14

Nathan woke up the next morning determined more than ever to get away from Maddie's clutches. She had a hold on him and it was not good. He was determined to get out of it any way he could. There was only one real way out of this mess, and that was to tell the truth to Anna and his classmates.

But how?

How could he possibly tell the truth now after all this time? His classmates would surely shun him, and Anna would never forgive him. There were too many holes in this plan, too many ways for it to backfire on him. He didn't like his odds, but at this point there was almost nothing else he could do to make things right.

So why did he feel so uneasy about it?

Probably because he knew that he stood to lose everything when the truth came out, especially Anna.

How could he possibly make this work and still keep everything in his life intact? The truth would come out one way or another, and it would be better coming from him than from Maddie. He needed to be sure that his classmates would not reject him when they learned the truth, but there was no way of gauging what their reaction would be. They would either shun him or welcome his honesty. It wasn't likely that his friends would be too accepting of the truth he'd been keeping from them for the past four years of high school. He didn't know why, but he wasn't ready to handle something this stressful.

The way things at school were now, he held the respect of his fellow students. If they were to find out that he'd been lying to them all along, he would never be able to face them again. It was likely that he would never see most of them again after graduation, but on the off-chance that he would have to encounter them again, he didn't want to ruin his chances for future relationships with any of them.

As for Anna, he would risk nothing short of everything to keep from hurting her more than he already had. This was the reason his parents had always impressed upon him to tell the truth. Lies seemed to multiply all on their own, and they usually ended up getting so out of control that they would never be manageable. It was too late to give himself a lecture on the perils of lying; he was already there.

The time to consider the risks of losing Anna had passed. At the point where the lies outweighed the truth, it was time to put an end to it, by whatever means possible. Anna would never understand his feelings about the Amish ways since she was brought up with most of them. She would never understand why he'd lied or why it embarrassed him for anyone to know his mother was Amish.

He'd considered going through the hassle of explaining that Lydia was not his birth mother, but then he would have to explain the rest of it. The part where his own father didn't even know of his existence until he was seven years old. That was something that Nathan had put behind him a long time ago, but he wasn't willing to risk ridicule over such a thing. Those kids who had been brought up with two parents all their lives would never understand his broken family situation.

He didn't know much about his classmates' personal home lives, and he preferred to keep it that way so as to keep his own family life private. It was an easy out, he knew, but as long as he never talked about anything too personal with them or asked questions about their lives, he was able to keep his own life private.

He preferred it that way.

Chapter 15

Maddie slid into the seat beside him in the auditorium once again.

"I'd like it if we could do more than cut pieces of fabric today. I'd like you to start teaching me those fancy stitches that your Amish girlfriend told me about," she whispered.

When he didn't answer, she leaned up and whispered in his ear. "Did you hear me, Amish Boy?"

It surprised him that he had no reaction to her. Was it possible that he was actually getting used to her presence? What did he really have to lose by continuing to teach her to quilt? He could teach her his stitches and be done with her, and Anna would never be the wiser.

Or, he could continue to ignore her and pray that she would go away. Now there was an idea; prayer. Maybe, because it was his own sin that had gotten him into this mess in the first place, that he'd feared asking God for help on the off chance that his prayer would go unanswered.

Though most of this mess was a means to protect his identity from his classmates, he realized almost by accident, it was to protect Anna and his family as well. After all, he was doing it for their own good, wasn't he? At least that's what he tried hard to convince himself. What he was doing was just as much for the privacy of his loved-ones as it was for himself.

He had seen far too many *Englischers* around town snapping pictures of the Amish, throwing things at them, and mistreating them in general just because they were different. He told himself that he was only trying to protect Anna and his family from suffering ridicule from the *Englisch.* So why did it feel like he was caught in the middle of the web of lies? Maybe because that was fact, and his public life was fiction. It was the truth, and he was refusing to face it.

It didn't matter which way he turned, there really was no way out of this situation and time alone would not fix this mess he'd gotten himself into.

Nathan turned to Maddie and spoke to her in a calm voice. "I will teach you the stitches today, but I expect you to stop calling me *Amish Boy,* or this deal we made is over."

He was firm, but authoritative. Maddie held a look of respect for a moment, but it left her quickly, her usual, disapproving look returning.

She reluctantly nodded.

If he could be sure that Maddie was satisfied with his teaching, and her quilt was well underway before they returned home, then he would be able to put this whole mess behind him and never worry about it again. After all that was what he really wanted more than anything.

But what he really wished at this point was that he had never come on this trip in the first place.

Nathan realized now that he didn't really belong here. He belonged at home in the Amish community, and that was where he would stay. He still intended to finish out the week and to take the seminar classes, but only so he could use that knowledge to provide for his wife-to-be. After he left here at the end of the week, he would never think about this place again, for it was a place he just didn't belong. He only wished that he would've realized this long before he'd left his family and Anna behind.

Chapter 16

Nathan sat across from Maddie studying her as she followed his instructions to the letter. The stitches were clumsy, yet surprisingly evenly spread. It was the first time that he dared to even look at her longer than a few seconds. All he could identify her with was the high ponytail that rested at her crown and cascaded in a spiral from the top of her head. That blond ponytail swung back and forth whenever she walked the halls at school and was a telltale sign that she was on the rampage about something. She'd become feared at their high school and that blond ponytail seemed to give her power.

Now as he sat across from her, he saw vulnerability in her eyes, as though she'd let her guard down just for a minute.

Nathan felt suddenly brave. "Why are you so mean all the time?"

Maddie looked up, surprise in her fiery green eyes. "It's expected of me," she said casually.

Nathan shook his head in disbelief.

"What do you mean it's expected of you?"

Maddie smiled. "Cheerleader equals mean girl. You do the math."

"But we are not at school right now. You don't have to be mean to me."

The corners of Maddie's mouth turned up in such a way that she almost looked more beautiful to him than he'd ever seen her.

"You naïve little Amish boy. Don't you know that if I'm not mean all the time I lose my position of power as cheerleader? Because they expect it from me, I must act a certain way or the other students don't respect me."

"I would certainly respect you more if you were nice." Nathan said.

Maddie looked up from her stitches and gave him a funny look. "Cheerleaders are highly competitive. If we aren't mean, we lose our edge."

Nathan snatched her sewing out of her hands and forced her to look at him. "Have you ever actually tried being nice? You might actually like it."

Maddie's face turned up into the meanest look he'd ever seen on her face. "Nice people are weak."

Nathan chuckled. "Who in the world told you that?"

Maddie tipped her head casually.

"Cheerleading coaches tell us all the time. They tell us not to be nice because it shows weakness. If we are mean and spiteful to everyone, it gives us power; the power to win."

Nathan couldn't believe what he was hearing. "Is it possible the coaches meant for you to apply that attitude toward the games and cheerleading competition and not toward your everyday lives? Life is not a cheerleading competition."

Maddie leaned forward and narrowed her eyes. "Life in general is a competition, Amish Boy."

"What exactly is it that you are competing for with me?"

The look on Maddie's face changed. Her eyes clouded over and her expression fell.

"I just want you to like me."

Nathan laughed heartily. "If you want me to like you, you can start by not calling me Amish Boy anymore. I would like you a whole lot better if you would lose the attitude."

"My attitude is expected of me. Without my attitude, I wouldn't feel like a cheerleader. I don't know how to be any other way since I've been so mean for so long. I've been mean for too long to change. I wouldn't know how to be nice."

"Then reinvent yourself. We're about to graduate high school, and you don't have to be the mean cheerleader anymore. Move on with your life and try something new."

“I'm supposed to be coming here on a cheerleading scholarship. Here in college I will probably have to be the meanest cheerleader in order to survive. All I ever wanted to do since I was a little girl is to be a cheerleader for the Hoosiers."

"What do you mean in order to survive?"

"If I'm not the meanest cheerleader, then the meanest one will overtake me. And I will never survive the squad. My goal is to be squad leader, and I can't do that by being nice."

Nathan looked at her with sympathy in his eyes. She was far more confused than he was about life and about who she was.

"Try being nice sometimes. You don't have to be nice during your cheerleading competitions or whatever, but try being nice as a human being to others. When you're kind to people, they are kind right back to you."

Maddie’s eyes turned sad. "I already told you…I've been mean so long I don't know how to be nice."

Nathan smiled. "You are being nice to me right now, and you didn't even realize it. You've gone five whole minutes without calling me Amish Boy. That's an accomplishment."

Maddie let out a half giggle, half cry. Tears welled up in her eyes, and she smiled brightly at him.

"You are right, Amish Boy."

Nathan chuckled. "See? When you say it like that, it doesn't hold the same meaning."

"I only said it because I don't really know your real name."

"My name is Nathan."

"It's nice to meet you, Nathan."

Nathan smiled.

He had won this round.

Chapter 17

When Maddie sat down next to him in the auditorium, Nathan actually didn't cringe.

"Hey, Nate."

No one had ever called him Nate before, and he kinda liked it.

"You're late, Maddie. I was beginning to think you weren’t going to show up today."

Maddie nudged him with her elbow. "And miss out on the chance to sit next to you all day? You can't get rid of me that easily."

"I was afraid of that," Nathan said chuckling.

Maddie nudged him in the arm again.

"Don't be so mean, Amish Boy."

"You know you're going to have to stop calling me that if we're going to be friends."

"If people found out I was friends with an Amish boy, it would ruin me."

Nathan smiled at her. "The only way they're going to know is if you tell them."

Maddie smile back. "You might be onto something, Nate."

After their lecture Maddie went to meet up with the cheerleading squad that she hoped to be a part of once she attended school here. They didn't have anything to do for a while, so he decided to go along and watch their cheering. On their last day here at the university, there was to be a special pep rally held, and Maddie was supposed to be a part of it. Now she was busy practicing for that cheer she would do with her new squad.

None of Nathan's friends were here with him, as none of them intended to attend here. They had all been accepted to out-of-state colleges. Maddie, in all her meanness, was the closest thing he had to having a friend here with him for the duration of their trip. He wasn't sure he would classify her as a friend just yet, but if she continued to let her guard down and be nice to him, it was a possibility.

Nathan sat on the bleachers watching Maddie interact with the other cheerleaders. Inside her element she was a whole different person, and he realized that she wasn't all that unlike him. He too was most in his element when he was quilting. She was right about one thing, cheerleaders were mean. He sat there watching them arguing back-and-forth, taking pot shots at each other. All they seemed to do was put each other down. Maddie flashed him a helpless look, and he felt sorry for her. He knew it was her dream to be a cheerleader, but she was going to have to decide if she could do that and be a nice person at the same time. He knew that wouldn't be an easy task for her, but with a little help from him, her new friend, perhaps it could be accomplished.

Perhaps they could help each other.

Chapter 18

By the end of the week, they had managed to finish more than half of Maddie's quilt. It actually turned out a lot better than he thought originally. Though they'd had to pull some of it apart and redo it because it didn't fit, in the end it all worked out. Now it was their last day at the University, and Nathan felt confident that Maddie could finish the quilt on her own without his help.

He would almost miss her, since they had become closer over the past few days. After finally letting her guard down, they had gotten along a lot better. He wasn't sure how things would be once they returned home, but he had a feeling she might go back to her old self once they got into school and around their classmates.

It bothered him to think such a thing, but he also knew how hard high school could be and the pressures that the cheerleaders were under. She shared a lot more with him about what goes on behind the scenes during cheerleading practice, and he did not envy her one bit. Her pressures were a lot more in depth than his ever could be. It saddened him that others couldn't just accept people for who they are, but he feared that that was the way of the world. It was one of the reasons he preferred the Amish community.

Nathan sat in the bleachers along with all the other students that had come for the tour and watched the pep rally giving them a send-off for the last day at the University. Nathan was sad it was his last day, but he was more than ready to go home and face whatever his future with Anna held. He'd already made up his mind before he'd even stepped foot on campus, but it wasn't until now, on his last day, that he realized that his future never included the university. It only included Anna, and teaching his own children someday how to quilt, so that they could carry on his legacy.

Although Nathan would be happy to go home, he would certainly miss this place. It was his only opportunity to experience college. He had enjoyed himself immensely while he was here. The freedom and the fun did not go unnoticed. But now it was time to grow up and face his future head-on. He had made a promise to Anna, and he would keep that promise because he loved her. He didn't mind sacrificing the college experience, for he got to have that for five whole days, and that was more than enough for him.

Even after that first, day he realized he didn't really belong here. He belonged at home with Anna and his family and his quilt shop that his *mamm* had so lovingly given to him. He packed his bag, preparing to leave all of this behind. He would never be a college student. He would forever be a quilter's son, and he was content with that.

Chapter 19

Anna prepared a light meal to take with her to the quilt shop today. She was expecting Nathan to show up around the lunch hour, and she hoped to surprise him with his favorite homemade banana bread and corned beef sandwiches with Swiss cheese. She was excited that they would share a meal together after being apart for an entire week. She was so excited to see him; she was almost nervous. It has been a long week waiting for him, and she was more than ready to have him home. She longed to hold him in her arms once again and shower him with the sweet kisses that he loved so much. She had never had the opportunity to miss him before, and this had been a new experience for her. They had talked every night on the phone, but it just wasn't the same. The first two days she hadn't spoken to him at all, and when she finally talked to him, his demeanor worried her a little bit.

Nathan had told her all about the college campus and shared with her how excited he was about all of it, and that worried her. She knew that he was part of an *Englisch* world that she was not part of, and she wondered if he would rather be there than here with her.

Anna's heart quickened at the jingle of the bells on the front door the quilt shop. In walked Nathan, looking more handsome than she'd ever seen him before, his sandy brown hair slicked back with hair gel, wearing a blue tie to complement his crisp white dress shirt. She stood abruptly, knocking the chair over behind her, but she didn't care.

Nathan scooped her up in his arms and twirled her. He pressed his lips to hers, and he'd never tasted a kiss so sweet. His mouth swept over hers hungrily. Oh, how he'd missed her. He drank in the flowery smell of her, and it tickled his senses. Nathan couldn't get enough of her. He pulled her as close as he could and didn't want to let her go ever again.

He'd missed her.

He missed her smell, the way she giggled, even the way she sighed sometimes whenever they were quiet together making a quilt. If he could spend the rest of his life kissing this woman, he'd be the happiest man on earth.

School didn't matter.

Nothing else mattered but this moment with her. He swept his mouth across her neck and whispered in her ear quietly. “I love you, my sweet Anna. I will never leave you again. I could hardly bear to be separated from you."

Anna breathed heavily, matching the fervor of his kisses with equal exertion. She had missed him so much, and now her hunger for him could not be satisfied. His lips were warm against hers. She felt his arm wrap around her lower back and pull her toward him. Warmth surged through her at his touch. She loved the way he held her so close, as if they were one. Being in his arms was home to her. She couldn't get enough of him, and she enjoyed his desire for her.

“I love you, my sweet Anna,” he whispered again.

He loved kissing her, but he was ready to be married to her so there could be more.

Chapter 20

Anna was so lost in Nathan's kiss, she thought she heard the bells of angels as if she'd died and gone to heaven.

"Nate honey, you left your bag on the bus."

Anna tore herself from Nathan's arms, whipping her head around toward the door of the quilt shop and the sound of the woman's voice. Before her, stood a beautiful young woman in a cheerleading outfit holding a white handled paper bag toward Nathan.

Anna looked at Nathan, fire in her eyes.

"Who is this," she said in a lowered voice. "And why is she calling you honey?"

Maddie took a step forward, tipped her head, and flashed a mean smile at Anna. "I'm his apprentice. He's teaching me how to quilt."

Anna looked at Nathan who was trying really hard not to look guilty.

"Since when?" Anna said through a nervous smile.

Maddie giggled. "Oh he didn't tell you about me?"

Anna gritted her teeth and pasted on a fake smile. "No, he hasn't said a word."

Anna extended a hand to Maddie as if she was afraid of catching germs. "I'm Anna. I'm engaged to be married to Nathan."

Maddie giggle. "Aww, no you're not."

Anna could feel her blood boiling as she turned to Nathan. "Did you tell her we are engaged?"

Maddie interrupted. "He already told me the truth about the two of you. We talked about it while he was teaching me to make my butterfly quilt."

Anna let out a screech and stormed off, stomping her feet against the wooden floor of the quilt shop. She ran into the bathroom and slammed the door shut and locked it. Feeling weak in the knees, Anna slid to the floor, her back against the door. She began to cry, tears choking her. All she could think about was Nathan betraying her with that pretty cheerleader.

Nathan tapped lightly on the door of the bathroom. "Anna come out here, please. I can explain."

Nathan could hear her muffled cries as she attempted to speak, but he couldn't understand a word she was saying.

Anna sniffled "How could you, Nathan? How could you make a butterfly quilt with that… that *cheerleader*?"

Nathan didn't want to converse with her with the door between them, and he certainly didn't want to talk to her about this when Maddie was within earshot of their conversation.

"Anna, please come out of there and I'll explain everything to you."

"Just go home," came her muffled sobs. "Go away and leave me alone. You have ruined everything."

Nathan pressed his ear to the door. He hated to hear her cry, especially when it was his fault.

"Anna, please let me explain."

"There's nothing left to say, Nathan. Go home."

Nathan stepped away from the door, the weight of his lies crushing his heart.

Chapter 21

"She won't talk to me," Nathan complained. "It's been three days."

Steve patted his son on the shoulder thoughtfully. "She'll come around. You just need to give her a little time."

Nathan leaned against the fence rail, removed his hat, and tossed it on the ground.

"She's never going to forgive me; I really screwed up."

"I know it's too late tell you now, but you should've stayed away from that cheerleader. Those cheerleaders will get you into trouble every time."

Nathan turned around and looked at his dad strangely. "Wasn't my birth mother a cheerleader?"

Steve chuckled. "Yes she was, Son. And she broke my heart."

Nathan shook his head. "You don't have to worry about me, dad. I don't think of Maddie that way. I love Anna."

Steve looked at his son sincerely. "I'm glad to hear that. If you sincerely love Anna, then you need to cling to her. You have to do whatever it takes to make this right. Trust me when I tell you, don't let too much time go by, or you might live to regret it. Don't repeat my mistakes, Son. I've had to live with a lot of regret over the years, and I'd like to spare you that. It's not a good way to live."

"What if she'll never forgive me?"

"That's the chance you have to take when you walk the honorable road. Pray about it, Son. God won't let you down."

Nathan knew his dad was right. Praying was the one thing he hadn't done in this situation yet.

Nathan set off on foot toward his Uncle Liam's farm across the 2 mile stretch of cornfield that separated their houses. He hoped he would find his grandfather at the *dawdi haus* so he wouldn't have to do much explaining to anyone else in the family. His Grandpa John, who had married his Grandma Nellie ten years ago, had become a great source of information regarding his birth mother. Grandpa John never judged him no matter what he said, and he was always a good listener. Grandma Nellie would make them Meadow tea during his visits, and they would often sit for hours while Nathan listened to Grandpa spout off one story after another about his birth mother.

This time, he needed some real-life advice, and he knew Grandpa John would be there to help without judgment. Right now, he needed to spill his guts, and if anyone would understand, it would be Grandpa John.

Chapter 22

Thankfully, it was late enough in the day that he found his grandfather just where he hoped; in the *dawdi haus*.

Grandpa John met him at the door and invited him into the small home adjacent to his Uncle Liam's farm. "I had a feeling I'd be seeing you soon, Nathan."

"Dad called you, didn't he?" he asked knowingly.

He told me about your argument with Anna, and I knew you would be around to see me soon enough."

Nathan sat down, and on cue, Grandma Nellie came over and hugged him before putting the tea kettle on the stove. He waited for her to leave the room so he could talk to his grandpa in private.

“I really screwed up this time, Grandpa."

John folded his hands across his lap and leaned back in his chair. “Does this have anything to do with you being accepted at the University?"

Nathan sat up straight, his heart pounding furiously. "How did you know about that?"

"I could see it in your eyes whenever you talked about the seminars you were taking there. I knew there had to be more to it than just taking seminars. I figured you got accepted, and you were touring the campus just to see what your options were."

"That's exactly what I did, Grandpa. But only I didn't tell Anna about it. But right now, that is the least of my troubles. She thinks I like Maddie, a girl from school, but I don't. I don't know how I can convince her."

John paused for a moment and then spoke. "What would make her think that you like Maddie?"

Nathan felt the guilt weighing on his heart. "Because I helped Maddie make a butterfly quilt. I let Maddie blackmail me into helping her with it. I knew it was wrong but I did it anyway because I was afraid. I was afraid that the kids at school would know that I've been raised Amish."

"And this Maddie? She was threatening to tell all your classmates about your home life?"

Nathan couldn't even look at his grandpa. He couldn't look him in the eyes. "I've never felt so ashamed in all my life. I don't know why I was afraid that if the kids at school knew I was brought up Amish they would tease me. I suppose it was because I've seen a lot of teasing of the Amish in town by some of the kids at school, and I didn't want that to happen to me. All I cared about was getting my education; I didn't think about how that was affecting my family or Anna. I tried to tell myself that I was doing it for the protection of Anna and even my *mamm*. It just wasn't the whole truth."

"There's nothing wrong with wanting to protect yourself from ridicule, Nathan. But when it involves you telling lies to others, that's when you need to draw the line."

"I know that now, but it's too late. The damage is already done."

John walked over to the stove, picked up the whistling tea kettle, brought it to the table, and filled their cups. "It's never too late to tell the truth."

Nathan lifted the steaming cup to his lips and blew on it to cool it. "I hope you're right, Grandpa."

John sat back down across from Nathan and looked at him thoughtfully. "Why don't you tell me about your tour of the campus? I'll be more than happy to help pay for your college, if that's what you want to do. I'll support you no matter what your decision is in this life."

Nathan shook his head. "I realized the first day of the tour that I don't belong there. I belong here with my family and with Anna. I want to marry her more than ever."

"Then I suggest you get over there in a hurry and make things right with her."

Nathan left after a few more minutes, but not without hugging his Grandma Nellie and thanking Grandpa John for another bout of great advice.

Chapter 23

Anna turned around as the bells jingled on the door to the quilt shop. She felt her emotions rise at the sight of the cheerleader. That girl was the last person Anna wanted to see today.

Anna toughened her expression. "He's not here, Cheerleader. So you can go home."

Maddie smiled. "Amish Girl has an attitude. I like that."

Maddie dared to sit down across from Anna. "I didn't come here to fight with you. I came here to apologize."

Anna sat at attention. "I'm listening. You've got one minute, Cheerleader."

"First of all, my name is Maddie. Maddie Hayes. I go to high school with Nathan. I was also on the tour of the IU campus with him."

Anna's ears perked up. "What do you mean you toured the campus?"

Maddie leaned in as if to tell her a secret.

"You mean he didn't tell you? We were there to tour the campus. Everyone who got accepted to the University was there."

Anna sat back in her chair feeling deflated. Her heart sank at the thought of Nathan being accepted to the college, but more than that, he had kept it from her.

"By the look on your face, I'd say he didn't tell you. I'm guessing he didn't tell you I was blackmailing him either?"

Anna's eyes widened. "Why were you blackmailing him? Better yet, why are you telling me all of this?"

Maddie looked away. "Because I don't want you to hate me. I don't have any real friends, and I'd like us to be friends."

Anna scoffed. "Aren't you already friends with Nathan?"

Maddie sighed. "Nate and I are not friends. I blackmailed him into helping me with the butterfly quilt.

I'm sure you don't remember me, but I was in here in this store a few months ago and asked you about quilting."

Anna studied Maddie for a moment. "I get a lot of customers in here, but I do remember you, now that you mentioned it. I told you about the butterfly quilt Nathan and I made when we were younger. Why were you so interested in making a butterfly quilt, yourself?"

Maddie cleared her throat nervously.

"Because I had a crush on Nate, and I was jealous of you," Maddie admitted.

Maddie's confession surprised Anna.

"I kind of figured you liked him, but why did you use that to blackmail him?"

"Maybe I should let him tell you the rest himself."

"It's a little too late for that, Maddie. If you want to gain my trust and be my friend like you say you do, then you'll tell me everything."

Maddie proceeded to tell Anna everything. It saddened Anna that Nathan felt the need to keep all of this from her. They were supposed to be married, but how could they do that if he couldn't even be honest with her?

"I wish I had known how he really felt. It upsets me that he seems to be ashamed of our relationship."

"Anna, he's not ashamed of you or your relationship. He's the exact opposite. He told me right from the very beginning that he was engaged to be married to you. That man loves you, and he was only trying to protect you."

"He doesn't seem to love me enough to trust me with his feelings." Anna's heart was broken. If not for her new friend's honesty, she probably would've never known the truth.

"Thank you, Maddie. I'd like us to be friends."

Maddie felt a lump form in her throat. She'd never had a real friend before.

"If we're friends, does that mean you will help me finish my quilt?"

Anna nodded and smiled. "I will be glad to help you."

Maddie was grateful for Anna's generosity, and for the friendship she offered. It made her want to be a nicer person.

Chapter 24

"Thank you for seeing me, Anna," Nathan said quietly. "I know I don't deserve anything from you right now, but I pray that you'll forgive me."

Anna felt her heart flutter. "Why didn't you think you could trust me with your feelings? We've known each other since we were little kids. I've always been completely honest with you."

"Since Maddie told you everything, I'm not sure there's anything more I can say, except that I really am sorry. I never meant to hurt you. I was trying to protect myself and my own feelings more than I was trying to protect you, and for that I'm very sorry."

"I've already forgiven you," she said quietly. "But it might be a while before I can trust you again."

Nathan sighed heavily. He knew it was going to be a lot of work to put his relationship with Anna back together. But he was prepared to do whatever it took to secure their future, the future he'd always planned for. "I understand. But please know that I love you."

Anna turned her back on him. "I think you should go to college if that's what you want to do."

Nathan stepped up behind her and wrapped his arms around her, tucking his face deep into the crook of her neck. He breathed in the sweet smell of meadow flowers. "I don't want to go to college. I want to stay here with you. I want to marry you, if you'll still have me."

Nathan kissed her softly on the neck, sweeping his mouth up to her ear and across her tense jawline.

Anna turned around, unable to resist him any longer. She pressed her lips against his, leaning into the kiss with more enthusiasm than she'd ever kissed him before. "I have loved you since I was a little girl," she whispered in between kisses. "And I will love you for the rest of my life."

"I love you too, Anna. And I'm ready to be a husband, and a provider, and a father when the time comes."

Anna pulled away from him slightly, resting in his loosened grasp. "What about your online quilting business?"

"I decided against it. Everything I have is right here with you. This quilt shop is where it all started for us, and I wouldn't want to change a thing."

Anna giggled. "I wouldn't either."

Nathan pulled her close again and pressed his lips to hers. He could spend the rest of his life kissing her; the rest of the world could wait.

The End of book 3

THE QUILTER'S SON

Maddie's Quilt

Book Four

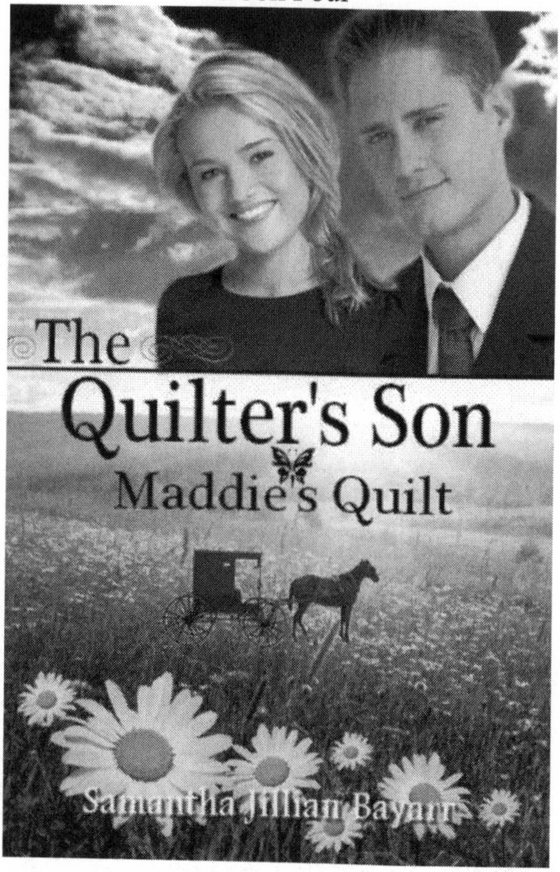

Samantha Jillian Bayarr

All scripture references in this book used from New International Version of the Bible

Chapter 1

"Oh, Maddie, are you sure?"

Maddie sat across from Anna at the kitchen table of the small home that her friend would be sharing with Nathan in less than two weeks. Nothing seemed real to Maddie. Even her thoughts were a struggle.

"I'm sure," she said quietly, choking back the sobs that threatened to expose her fear. "I saw a doctor at the clinic just off campus."

"Do you have a plan? How are you going to take care of a baby and finish school?"

Maddie couldn't hold her emotions any longer; she began to sob. "I have no plan! The cheerleading coach told me to *take care of it*, or I can't come back to the squad. I understand that they can't allow a pregnant cheerleader to remain on the squad, but if I keep it, I'm going to lose my cheerleading scholarship. My grades are not good enough to keep me in school."

Anna looked at Maddie, trying not to think the unthinkable.

“Oh, Maddie, what are you saying? You wouldn’t *take care of it* like that, would you?”

Maddie lowered her head.

“Of course not! I could never do that,” she sobbed.

Anna stood, went over to her friend, and hugged her closely. Maddie’s shoulders shook with anguish.

"My parents told me I couldn't come home," Maddie said, crying even harder. “They said I’ve ruined my life! They’re right! I’ve been at school less than three months, and I’m already pregnant. A baby isn’t supposed to ruin your life; it’s supposed to bring joy. But I’m so terrified; I have no idea how I’m going to do this alone.”

"What about the baby's father?" Anna asked gently. "Is he planning on marrying you?"

Maddie cried even harder, if that was possible. "I was so stupid. I really thought he liked me. I didn't mean for things to go that far, especially since we were at a party and there were other people around. But I was careless enough to follow him to one of the private rooms upstairs so we could have a quiet conversation.

He wanted to do everything *except* talk, and I didn't stop him! I found out later that I was one of many conquests for him that night. So, no, he isn't going to marry me. I didn't know where else to go, but I was afraid you would turn me away too."

Anna continued to comfort her friend through her sobs. She had no right to judge Maddie, given the magnitude of the *mistake* she had just made recently.

"If he isn't going to marry you," Anna said. "Then you will stay here with me."

Maddie looked at up Anna, whose face held sincerity.

"I can't live here. You and Nate are about to be married. The last thing two newlyweds need is a pregnant friend underfoot; I'll only be in the way."

Anna shook her head. "I can't let you sleep out in the cold. And I'm not going to let you end your pregnancy just to keep that cheerleading scholarship. We will figure something out. In the meantime, you can stay in one of the spare rooms and you can work with me at the quilt shop. Nate has been looking for someone to hire, and you'll be perfect for the job."

Maddie wiped her face with the back of her hand and hiccupped, her shoulders shuttering.

"What would I ever do without your friendship?"

Anna gave Maddie one last squeeze, and then sat back down across from her at the table.

"You are not going to have to find out. Now let me show you to the spare room, and we will get you settled in."

Maddie followed Anna down a short hallway toward a small bedroom with plain furnishings. Her surroundings didn't matter so much as where she was. Anna would help her through this; that much Maddie knew for sure.

Suddenly her situation didn't seem quite as scary; Anna would be there with her every step of the way. For the first time since the doctor had given her the news, she felt hopeful that everything would work out, for she had the comfort of a good friend to get her through it.

Chapter 2

"Are you sure I don't look stupid?" Maddie asked, looking down at the hemline of the dress Anna was sewing for her.

"I have to admit, you look a bit Amish, but you don't look stupid," Anna said with a little giggle.

Maddie pulled away from Anna, who was busy pinning the hem of the dress. "I don't want to look Amish. I'm not sure I'm ready for this just yet."

Anna folded her arms and raised an eyebrow at her friend. "Your clothes are getting too tight, Maddie, and you need to accept that you must wear bigger clothes. You're having a baby! You should be happy."

Maddie teared up. "That's easy for you to say. You are about to be married; I'm never going to get a husband. You don't know how I feel, because it would be okay for you to be pregnant."

Anna felt her stomach turn. She'd suspected for three weeks now that she was in the same spot as Maddie, but she was hoping it wasn't so.

"Who says it's not okay for you to be pregnant?" she asked Maddie, trying to hide her own shame. "God has blessed you with that child, and you should be happy with it. I know your circumstances aren't what you want them to be, but God will bring someone into your life, who will love that baby as if it was his own."

Anna wished she could take the same advice she was now trying her best to convince Maddie of, but it was next to impossible.

Maddie swiped at a teardrop on her cheek.

"I hope you're right. And I hope it happens soon. I really don't want to do this alone."

Anna hugged her friend, feeling some of the same worries. "It will happen all in God's timing. That you can count on."

Maddie slumped down into a chair. "Look at me," she said as she ruffled the skirt of the dress she was wearing. "No man is going to want to marry me when I'm already pregnant."

Anna sat across from Maddie at the kitchen table wondering the same thing for herself as she took a sip of her tea. "I happen to know that Nathan's cousin, Elias, has shown an interest in you. He knows you're pregnant, and he's still interested."

Maddie laughed nervously. "He's Amish."

"You don't want to go out with him just because he's Amish?" Anna asked.

"His being Amish has nothing to do with it. Well, it does have something to do with it. I mean, because he's Amish he would probably be all honorable and marry me. But if I'm going to consider marrying an Amish man, I would rather go for Nate's cousin, Seth, instead. But I'm not so sure I would want to be with either of them just for the sake of not having to raise this child alone."

Anna tried not to let her emotions show.

"You wouldn't go out with Elias just to avoid being alone. And, yes, he would probably eventually ask to marry you, but what's wrong with that?"

Maddie sniffled and giggled at the same time. "Nothing I suppose. But I have to admit, Seth is quite handsome, and I'd rather you asked him." She didn't dare speak of the one she *really* wanted, for she would never hurt Anna that way.

Anna forced a smile. "Then it's settled. I'll have Nathan ask Seth to take you for a buggy ride. But he can ask Elias first, since he's the one who's interested."

Maddie patted her stomach. "I don't think it would help my reputation too much if I went out with two, so let's start with Seth."

Anna struggled to keep her emotions in check. "I'll have Nathan ask him tomorrow."

Maddie felt a funny twinge in her gut. It wasn't that she despised the idea of dating Seth, but it made her feel surprisingly unsettled knowing Nate would be doing the asking on her behalf. Seth might eventually want to marry her, and she just wasn't sure if she could love him the way a wife should.

Anna was right about one thing; Maddie needed to get out of the house and move on with her life. If she didn't, she feared the inappropriate feelings for Nate that had resurfaced since she'd come to live with Anna would increase, and it was growing more difficult each day to be around him. She knew it was due in part to her condition that made her yearn for what her friend had, but she had to keep those feelings in-check, for the sake of her friendships.

Maddie could never admit it, but she envied Anna.

Chapter 3

Nathan could never admit it, but he felt a little funny asking Seth to date Maddie. Was it possible that his feelings went far beyond friendship for her? It was too sinful to even think about.

He tried hard to convince himself that it was because he cared about her and wanted to protect her from being hurt anymore, but he wasn't so sure that was the only reason. He had thought he had feelings for Maddie since before they'd finished their tour of IU, feelings that had increased over the summer before she'd left for the Fall term. As soon as she'd gone away to school, he vowed to put her out of his mind and heart. He loved Anna, and would go through with his plans to marry her. He was committed to Anna and refused to allow himself to explore his feelings for Maddie.

Now he feared what would happen if he didn't sever his ties with Maddie, and handing her over to Seth would be a good start. For Anna's sake, he hated to purge Maddie from their lives, but he thought it best for the sake of his upcoming marriage.

"God give me the strength to overcome this," he whispered.

Nathan walked into the barn and spotted his cousin, Seth. It was now or never, and his future marriage depended upon a union between Seth and Maddie. He would help that happen if it meant he would have peace of mind and a solid marriage.

Seth looked up from the harness he was repairing and welcomed his cousin. "It's *gut* to see you, Nathan. Are you here on business?"

Nathan swallowed back anguish, fully determined to make things right for Maddie. "I'm here to ask a favor. I was wondering if you would consider taking an interest in Maddie."

Seth shrugged. "She's pregnant, by an *Englischer, jah*?"

"Yes, she is," Nathan said, swallowing hard. "That is why I came to you. She needs a husband."

Seth turned his attention back to his harness repair. "I'm not certain I would consider taking on a pregnant *fraa*. Are you sure she would be interested in me? She's beautiful!"

Seth knew he was making excuses, but he couldn't share the real reason for his resistance.

Nathan cleared his throat, searching for words that would make sense even to him. The thought of Maddie being interested in Seth pricked his heart. He didn't want it to affect him this way, but he just couldn't help his feelings. Nathan took a deep breath. "She's more than just beautiful. She's a hard worker, she can quilt, and she's a good person. You won't be disappointed."

Seth chuckled. "You sound like you are trying to sell me horse."

Nathan sighed impatiently. "Will you take her out for a buggy ride or not?"

Seth slighted his eyes toward Nathan and raised an eyebrow in question. "Why is this so important to you? It almost sounds like you are trying to get rid of her. But why?"

Nathan cleared his throat. "I'm just trying to look out for her. I want her to be happy."

That much was fact, but he didn't dare speak out loud his true feelings over the situation.

“Well if you ask me, dear cousin, there's more to it than that."

“Will you do it or not?" Nathan asked impatiently.

Seth stopped what he was doing, put the harness aside, and concentrated on his conversation with Nathan. He crossed his arms over his chest and looked deep into his cousin’s eyes for a clue of what he hoped for.

It never came.

"You have feelings for Maddie, don't you?" Seth accused him.

Nathan clenched his jaw and looked away.

"I am marrying Anna, and I won't discuss this any further with you."

“Did I strike a nerve, dear cousin?"

Nathan was growing tired of the conversation, especially since he couldn't control his emotions where Maddie was concerned.

"Maddie needs a husband, and I can't be that for her because I've promised to marry Anna. Are you interested in marrying Maddie or not?"

Seth chuckled again. "Who wouldn't be? Pregnant or not, she’s a catch for any man. But I'm not so sure I would be the one she'd be interested in, if you know what I mean."

"No I don't know what you mean," Nathan said gruffly.

"If you ask me, I think the two of you would rather be together."

Nathan narrowed his eyes at his cousin.

"No one asked you."

Nathan turned and walked away, unable to take his cousin's accusations anymore, no matter how much truth was behind them.

Chapter 4

Seth had no idea why he'd just agreed to go out with Maddie and possibly marry her, but he hoped to use that date as leverage to bring Anna to her senses. If it caused her to become jealous, thinking he could be interested in someone else, then he would take that chance.

After she'd broken things off between them, he'd been so miserable, and hadn't even considered another woman. Their brief, deceitful relationship had not lasted longer than the summer, but he'd thought she'd wanted to marry him instead of his cousin. It had begun after the fight she'd had with Nathan about his going to the college for a week, but soon after his cousin returned home, she'd tried to break it off between them. Every time she would try to end it, he would always manage to get her to see him just one more time. As the summer ended, her visits became less frequent until they dropped off altogether.

One day, after not seeing her for nearly a week, she'd told him to leave her alone. She'd said their brief relationship had been a shameful mistake and that she was determined to marry Nathan. Seth loved her enough to let her go, but he'd held out hope she would come to her senses and return to him. With less than two weeks before she was scheduled to marry his cousin, Seth was not above making one last gesture to assure he wouldn't have to live with regret over losing her for the rest of his life. He had fallen in love with her, even if she hadn't returned those feelings.

Anna wrung her hands the entire time Nathan was gone. What had she done? Was she truly ready to face her feelings for the two men she loved? If not for that argument she'd had with Nathan last spring, she would've never even considered another man. But when she felt Nathan drift away from her, she had turned to Seth for comfort. She had not planned on falling in love with Seth, nor had she ever dreamed she could've made the mistake she had, but now it was too late to turn back time.

How could she be in love with two men?

It was too shameful to even think about.

She had to find a way to tell Nathan and Seth the truth before it was too late. She couldn't let Seth marry Maddie without telling him how she felt about him. She knew she was being selfish, but the time to think about that had long since passed. Now, she had to put a stop to that date before things went too far between Seth and Maddie. She was set to marry Nathan in just a few days, but she could no more go through with that than she could continue hiding behind her lies.

Anna couldn't even look Maddie in the eye, knowing what she was about to do to her. She was about to crush her friend who needed a husband, but she could not let go of Seth.

Not now.

Anna's stomach churned, and she felt as if her breakfast would make its way back up. She couldn't ignore the obvious any longer, and she had to tell Seth before it was too late. She stood to lose everything because of her lies. Maddie would certainly hate her for taking away her only chance of having a husband, and Nathan would surely never speak to her again. She had betrayed him, and things would never be the same. How could she have thought that she could ignore what had happened between her and Seth? Now, nature was forcing her to come forth, and she was terrified.

She was a fool to think that she could still go through with marrying Nathan after all that had happened. Things had not been the same between them since he'd left for his college tour, and had become increasingly strained between them after he'd returned from school. He'd seemed agitated most of the time, and she feared he knew of her indecent behavior. If he had, he'd never said a word to her. As far as she knew, he still planned to marry her, but she could no longer go on hurting him. She'd been selfish, that much was certain, and now she faced losing everyone in her life she loved.

Chapter 5

Anna, you've been acting moody all day," Maddie complained. "Are you mad at me for some reason?"

Anna shook her head and went about the task of washing the evening dishes. Being Saturday, Maddie was dreading the buggy ride she was to take with Seth. He was expected to arrive in less than an hour, and Maddie regretted agreeing to go through with such a foolish plan. She knew he was taking her for a buggy ride that would most likely end with him asking for her hand in marriage, and she just wasn't ready for that. It wasn't like Nathan had stepped up and rescued her from her impending plight, but part of her foolishly held out hope that he would do just that so she wouldn't have to agree to Seth's proposal.

Anna continued to ignore Maddie, and it was beginning to upset her. Had she done something without knowing that it upset Anna? Maddie picked up the rinsed dishes and began to wipe them dry, while Anna stood next to her in silence, scrubbing furiously at a sauce pan.

Maddie grew impatient when Anna still did not answer her. "Are you mad at me, Anna?"

Anna didn't even look up from her chore.

"No! I'm mad at myself."

Maddie was confused. "How can you be mad at yourself? What did you do?"

"It doesn't matter anymore," Anna said, her voice breaking.

Maddie set down the plate she was drying and touched Anna's arm. "You're not making any sense Anna. What is wrong?"

"I can't talk about it. It's too horrible," Anna said, choking back sobs.

Maddie pulled her into a hug. "Getting pregnant without a husband was the most horrible thing I could have told anyone, but I told *you.* Surely whatever you have to say is not as bad as that."

Anna couldn't help but think that it was *exactly* like that.

"You'd be surprised," she said.

Maddie looked at her thoughtfully. "Maybe if you talk about it, it will help."

Anna sniffled. "I need to talk to Nathan first before I lose my nerve."

Maddie's mind began to reel. Was Anna planning on breaking things off with Nate? She knew it was wrong to hope for such a thing, but she just couldn't help her feelings. She dreaded the thought of watching Nate marry Anna, but she'd already agreed to be an attendant for the wedding. Maddie felt like the worst friend in the world, but she couldn't help that she loved Nate.

Maddie shivered as she watched light snowflakes flutter outside the kitchen window. It was going to be a long night in the cold with a man she didn't love. She was miserable and sad, at a time when she should be the happiest she could ever be.

Maddie stood staring out the window lost in thought. Her mind drifted to that hot August afternoon when Nate had nearly kissed her. They had stood so close to one another, and when he leaned, she leaned. She had felt his hot breath against her cheek as she let her eyes drift closed, but when the kiss never came and she opened her eyes, he'd skittered to the other side of the barn.

They never spoke about their close encounter, but Maddie often wished they had. Although she longed to kiss him, she didn't hold out much hope that it would ever come to pass, and so she regularly replayed that near-kiss in her mind, even though it usually brought her great sadness.

She had really messed up her life, and she worried her decision regarding Seth was about to mess up her child's life too.

Chapter 6

Seth pulled his buggy around to the side of his cousin's house. He was both dreading and looking forward to tonight. Dreading it because he didn't want to hurt Maddie, and looking forward to it so he could have the chance to see Anna and see her reaction. He wasn't trying to hurt Anna; he was hoping to get some sort of sign from her that she loved him. If not, he would go through with his proposal for Maddie. He hoped Maddie would make a good *fraa* and figured she would probably make him happy enough, but he wished Anna would come to her senses and take him back.

Maddie seem to be a good person and didn't deserve to be his second choice. He was determined to do right by her only for the sake of her child, but he wasn't sure that was enough.

Seth took a deep breath before knocking on the door. He would have to put his feelings for Anna aside since it was obvious that she knew about his meeting with Maddie.

He could hardly regret the mistake that he and Anna had made because he loved her deeply, but it was obvious that she had not returned that love, at least not enough to choose him over his cousin.

When he had proposed to Anna at the end of the summer, she had refused him, and it had hurt him deeply. Now he would have to face that rejection all over again when he picked up Maddie.

If it were up to him, he would marry Anna, but her bond with Nathan was too strong. His relationship with Anna, brief as it was, was sadly not strong enough to cause her to choose him.

Anna opened the door and let her gaze fall upon on Seth. He could tell she had been crying by the pink frames around her eyes, and he had to fight the urge to pull her into his arms and comfort her.

"Maddie will be ready in just a minute," she said with downcast eyes.

Seth reached for her, but she pulled away.

"Are you ever going to talk to me?" Seth asked desperately.

"I think the fact that you are here to escort Maddie for a buggy ride and ask her for her hand in marriage says everything that needs to be said, which is nothing," Anna said, fighting back tears.

"You don't understand, Anna."

Anna looked up at Seth, remorse in her eyes. "I understand absolutely everything. There is nothing more to say."

Anna regretted the words as soon as they left her lips. She wanted to lose herself in the shelter of his arms and let loose the words of love that choked her. She loved him; she'd been fooling herself for some time now about her feelings for Nathan. She and Nathan had been together for so long that she hadn't really realized when she'd stopped loving him, but she had. They had drifted apart but remained friends for so long that she was convinced she needed to keep to their plan.

She was to marry Nathan, and that was the plan. Nathan was safe while Seth excited her, and that scared her more than anything. Anna wasn't comfortable with change. But would she really have gone through with marrying Nathan just to avoid those exciting and scary changes in her life?

Now she was the most scared she'd ever been in her entire life. Scared of losing Seth forever, and scared of the possibility of raising a child on her own. Because of her foolishness, she was now facing being alone while Maddie married the one she truly loved.

She had to do something, but what?

She couldn't just blurt it all out, especially when she wasn't sure about her condition. Did she really want Seth to take her back simply because she was possibly pregnant? Anna thought about it for a moment. Wasn't that exactly what he was about to do for Maddie? Anna had seen on Maddie's face and sensed her agitation that she no more wanted to marry Seth out of obligation, than Anna herself would want the same for her and her baby. Yet here she was about to step aside and let Maddie walk out the door with the man she loved.

"God, please help me," Anna whispered.

Anna excused herself from Seth's company and walked toward the back of the house to look for Maddie. She found her in the bathroom hanging her head over the sink, sweat rolling down the sides of her face.

Anna quickly closed herself in the bathroom with Maddie "Are you alright?"

Maddie groaned." I don't think I can do this. Tell Seth I'm sick and I can't go tonight. Tell him I'm sorry."

Anna didn't need to be told twice. She nodded to Maddie before leaving the bathroom swiftly, a feeling of hope in her heart. Anna said a quick prayer of thanks just before she entered the living room where Seth was waiting. She looked in his eyes as she told him Maddie was sick and had to cancel the buggy ride, and she could've sworn that she saw relief in his expression.

Chapter 7

Anna couldn't look the cashier in the eye as she paid for the home-pregnancy test-kit. Her face had burned with humiliation as the woman seemingly took her time scanning the test-kit before hiding it away in a paper sack; she could feel the cashier's eyes boring a hole into her soul and it embarrassed her to her very core. She only wished she didn't have to find out the truth this way. She was certain that everyone in the store knew of her indiscretion; they seemed to all be staring at her.

No matter how much shame she felt at the moment, it was time she knew the truth once and for all. She'd been speculating and wondering for too many weeks, and it was time. Knowing the truth would be the least of her troubles since she already suspected as much. The tough part was going to be in telling Seth and her parents. Anna had no idea how she would even broach the subject with them. She feared Seth would reject her in the same way she had rejected his proposal.

Because of her foolishness, she feared she may have lost Seth forever. Her parents were a whole different story; they would surely shun her, even though Mennonite families were not usually that strict.

Anna drove her car slowly down the lane toward the house that was to be hers and Nathan's once they were married. In her haste to be wed, she'd already moved into the quaint little home that stood at the back end of his father's property.

As she pulled up to his home, she felt more out of place than she had when she'd moved in at the end of the summer. She wondered if she should just pack and move out. She knew she would have to eventually move out whether she got back together with Seth or not. There was no way she could follow through with marrying Nathan at this point. Even if she wasn't pregnant, she was still in love with Seth, and she had no right to hurt Nathan by marrying him now.

She certainly had no right to be living in his house.

But where was she going to go? She hadn't thought that far ahead. She couldn't go home. Her parents would be ashamed of her when they found out what she'd done. They would be further disappointed in her for her indiscretion with a man that was not her betrothed.

They might even disown her.

She supposed she would deserve as much.

She had really messed things up for her life and her child's life.

Anna cried out to God. "Please forgive me for my sins. Please put forgiveness in my parent's hearts and Seth's heart for what I've done. I love Seth, and I want to marry him. Please help me to put my life back together."

Anna felt peace wash over her as if her prayer had been answered. She was suddenly clear, and knew exactly what she needed to do, even if the outcome was not what she hoped for.

Chapter 8

Anna paced the floor of the bathroom, waiting for what seemed like a small lifetime. The kit said it would only take a few minutes, but she hadn't dared to look at it yet. She knew once she looked, whatever the answer was would be her fate, and there would be no taking it back.

A thousand thoughts crowded her mind. The one dominating thought was to tell Seth the truth about everything. She would tell him how she felt no matter what the test showed, and she would pray he could forgive her. She loved him, and she could only hope that he would return that love.

Anna's thoughts clouded over as she recalled her first kiss with Seth. She'd been standing on the bank of Goose Pond, trying to reach the cattails that grew among the long reeds.

It was dusk, and fireflies lit up the tall plumes, making them irresistible to her. Reaching a little too far, Anna had felt herself slip toward the water, until a strong arm looped around her waist and saved her from soaking herself. Thinking it had been Nathan who'd pulled her back on the bank, she'd turned her head and planted a kiss on the lips of her rescuer. When she realized it wasn't Nathan, she so was lost in Seth's kiss that she didn't want it to end. But he'd pulled away from her after a minute and asked her if she was sure of what she was doing. She'd nodded dreamily and pressed her lips against his once more. For some time she'd known she had feelings for Seth, but she had pushed them aside since she was already promised to Nathan.

That kiss had changed everything for her. Though she'd known Seth had loved her at one time, she'd pushed him away, feeling guilty over breaking her promise to Nathan. They'd been promised to one another since they were fourteen years old. But things had changed last summer.

After that first kiss, it hadn't mattered to Anna that she'd made a promise four years earlier to Nathan. She had fallen in love with Seth somewhere along the way, and there was no stopping those feelings, no matter how much she tried to push Seth away.

A tear rolled down Anna's cheek. She had loved Seth enough to allow him to compromise her virtue that stormy afternoon in the hayloft of his barn. But afterward, the more Seth had clung to her, the more she'd pushed him away. Why was she so afraid to let herself love him? Had it been because of her promise to Nathan, or had she felt too much shame over her love for Seth? Whatever the reason, she was now more terrified than ever that her love for him would not be enough to make up for breaking things off with him. She'd hurt him deeply the day they'd shared what would be their final kiss. Now, as she anticipated the results of her test, she prayed it had *not* been the last kiss she would ever have with Seth.

Anna peered over the sink and looked for the test results and her breath caught in her throat.

The only difference was…now she knew.

Chapter 9

Today is the day, Anna thought, as she forced her feet onto the cold, hardwood floor of the bedroom she would soon be leaving. Instead of pulling up the butterfly quilt that had meant so much at one time, she ripped it from the bed, realizing it had lost its meaning for her and Nathan. It was a symbol of their friendship, nothing more. The bed would never be *their* marriage bed.

Feeling suddenly queasy, just as she had for the past few weeks, she ran to the bathroom. Maddie was in front of the sink brushing her teeth, but Anna didn't care; worry over humiliation had long-since left her. Anna plunked down on the seat of the toilet and grabbed the wastebasket.

Her stomach heaved, but nothing came up.

She felt dehydrated.

Feeling Maddie's hand brush gently across her back, her stomach heaved a second time.

"If I didn't know any better, I'd wonder if you were pregnant too," Maddie said quietly. "But I know you and Nathan are waiting until you are married to have *relations.*"

"Nathan waited, but I didn't," Anna admitted, her face still hovering over the waste basket.

Maddie's eyes clouded over with worry.

"Oh, Anna, what are you saying?"

Anna pulled the stick from the waste basket that still boasted the tell-tale *plus sign* and showed it to Maddie.

Anna choked back tears as Maddie looked at her wide-eyed. "If not Nate, then who?"

Maddie would never admit that she felt relief that the child Anna carried did not belong to Nate. She almost didn't care who the father was, but knowing it wasn't Nate made all the difference in the world to her.

Anna dry heaved once more into the basket and then set it down on the floor. She grabbed a tissue and used it to wipe the bile from her lips.

"I'd rather not say just yet," she said. "I should probably have a talk with the baby's father first. I've hurt him, and I have a lot of explaining to do."

Maddie nodded, feeling guilty that her mind was reeling with thoughts of Nate being a free man. But then, her hand mindlessly went to her swelling middle, and she realized that even with Anna out of his life, Nate would never choose her. He would be hurt by Anna's actions, to say the least, but even that would not cause him to turn to her.

"My first plan of action will be to move out of Nathan's house," Anna said, sniffling. "I can't believe I thought that I could just marry him and push my feelings aside for..."

It suddenly made sense to Maddie. The looks that she thought she'd imagined between Seth and Anna had to have been real.

"It's Seth, isn't it?" Maddie said with a spurt of energy in her tone.

"How did you know?" Anna asked with a hiccup.

"I saw the tense looks the two of you exchanged last week when he came over to the house with Nate. It was obvious that something was going on between the two of you, but I pushed it aside, thinking you disliked him. Don't you wonder if Nate has noticed the same thing?"

Anna hadn't thought about it before, but she supposed there could be some truth to what Maddie was saying. What if he *had* noticed? Wouldn't he have said something to her by now if he had, or would he remain silent to protect her honor?

Her honor.

That was no longer in-tact.

"I'm not very good at hiding my emotions, I suppose," Anna said. "I don't know what to do about Nathan. I don't want to hurt him."

"The truth would probably be a good place to start," she said to Anna.

Maddie felt guilty that she had no words of comfort for her friend, but all she could think about was Nate and how this would affect him. Regret filled her as she ran her hand across her abdomen. Why hadn't she waited for God to choose her path in life? She had messed up her chance to have the man she truly loved, and there was nothing she could do about it now.

Chapter 10

Maddie spread out the butterfly quilt on Nate's bed, a lump of regret invading her throat. She felt foolish for placing her quilt on the bed the way she was, but she just wanted to see how it would have looked if she had been lucky enough to be his wife. She traced the pattern with her fingers, reliving every stitch and remembering every conversation she and Nate had had while piecing together the quilt.

It was then that she had fallen in love with him, but when they had returned from their school tour, her heart had broken from the realization of his relationship with Anna. She had spent the summer yearning for him, despite the knowledge of his commitment to Anna. When she had returned to school her heart was so utterly broken that she had turned to the first man who had paid any attention to her. That one irresponsible decision had cost her the only man she could ever truly love.

Tears filled her eyes and regret clouded her emotions as she continued to run her hand lovingly across the quilt. She was so caught up in the emotion of it that she didn't hear Nate walk in the house.

Nate stepped up to the doorway of his room, just in time to witness Maddie fingering the quilt they had made together. The dim, late afternoon sunlight reflected sorrow on her face, and he couldn't help but admire her beauty. Her golden hair shined with the specks of sunlight that filtered in through the sheer curtains at the window. Anna's quilt no longer graced the bed, and it momentarily confused Nate as to why Maddie's quilt was in its place. He couldn't help but think to himself how right it seemed and not out of place at all. Strangely, it almost didn't matter to him, but he had to know what had happened.

Nate cleared his throat. "Where is Anna?" he asked.

Startled out of her reverie, Maddie turned around to face Nate. Her hand instinctively grasped the quilt and began to pull it from the bed, but Nate put his hand down to stop her.

"Leave it there Maddie," he said softly.

Maddie looked at him curiously. "Anna is gone, and I'm all packed."

"I had a feeling she was going to leave," Nate said. "But I don’t understand why you feel the need to leave too. Your quilt can stay Maddie, and you can stay as well."

Maddie unclenched her fist that grasped the edges the quilt and smoothed it back over the bed.

"You want me to stay in here? This was to be your marriage bed with Anna."

How could he explain to her what he was feeling for her when he didn't even understand it himself? He had no right to pull her into his arms despite the urgency he felt, for he was not yet free from his obligation to Anna. It took every ounce of self-control to resist her.

"Anna didn't belong here," he finally said. "I think I've known that for some time."

Nate turned to leave, hoping to avoid the temptation to comfort Maddie. At the doorway he turned his head over his shoulder to look at her once more. "Please unpack your things. You are welcome to stay."

Maddie closed the space between them and wrapped her arms around his neck, pulling him close to her. Nate couldn't help folding his arms around her and pulling her close, for nothing had ever felt so right. He could stand to hold her forever, but he didn't dare let her know yet how he was feeling about her. He had pushed his feelings aside for so many months it had ended up hurting them both. He blamed himself for her condition. If he had not rejected her just before she'd left for school, he might have been able to spare her the sorrow that was now obvious.

"I have to go talk to Anna," he whispered in her ear. "But I will return later to bring in wood for the fireplace. It's going to be cold tonight and you will need to stay warm in your condition."

My condition.

Maddie didn't want to be reminded that she was carrying the child of a man she didn't love, while she was yearning for the one that would probably never be able to love her back. It was a fact, and he'd said it, and it hung in the air taunting her.

Maddie nodded as Nate pulled away from her.

She didn't mind bringing in the wood herself, but she would not turn down an opportunity to visit with him when he returned. Maddie's heart sang with new hope when she mirrored Nate's smile just before he exited the room. He had not been upset by her boldness in placing her quilt upon his bed. Instead he had welcomed her and invited her to stay.

Was it possible he was willing to take care of her despite her present condition? Or did he intend to go and win back Anna? She prayed that was not so, especially since he seemed to be accepting of Anna's absence in his home. Still, she couldn't help but allow hope to creep into her heart that Nate could possibly love her even half as much as she loved him.

Chapter 11

Anna stood just outside the barn, waiting for Seth to meet her. Though she shivered from the cold, she feared going inside and seeing the hayloft. That barn carried too many memories. Her hand naturally went to her abdomen as she tried to put the image of that indulgent afternoon out of her mind. It was difficult for her to think of that day as a mistake since she now carried a child made from the love that she and Seth shared that day. But she couldn't quite push aside the shame she felt for not waiting for marriage.

Anna's heart quickened its pace as Seth exited the barn. He pulled off his black felt hat and pushed sweaty blond hair off his forehead before replacing it. He worked hard. It was something she'd admired about him. After his parents had passed three years ago, he'd taken over the family farm and finished raising his two younger siblings. He was a nurturing sort of man, and she prayed his caring heart would extend to her after she told him what she'd come to say.

Anna sighed, unable to look Seth in the eye. She wrung her hands as she struggled for words to excuse her selfish behavior. Honesty was the only way out of this mess.

"*Mei schweschder* told me she saw you at the quilt shop earlier," Seth began. "She said you would be coming to see me this afternoon."

"I hope you don't mind that Rachel and I are friends."

Seth suppressed the urge to pull her into his arms. "*Nee,* she can remain friends with you even if you want nothing more to do with me."

Anna couldn't help but notice the sorrowful tone in his voice. This was going to be far more difficult than she'd imagined.

"I wanted to talk to you about…our relationship," she said quietly.

Seth blew out a deep breath, the warm vapor creating a thick cloud in front of him. "I believe you've already said all there is to say, Anna. You've made it very clear that our relationship is over."

"I made a mistake, Seth. I'm sorry for pushing you away and telling you it was over. I wish I could take it all back, but I can’t. All I can do is ask you to forgive me."

Confusion distorted Seth’s expression.

"That’s why you wanted to see me? To clear your conscience? You are days from marrying *mei* cousin. You’ve made your decision. Go back to Nathan’s *haus*."

His jaw clenched, and she could see he struggled to keep his composure.

Anna’s eyes filled with tears. "I moved out of Nathan’s house. I cannot work at the quilt shop anymore, and now I suppose I’m going to have to move back home with my parents."

Seth’s expression turned hopeful. "Have you called off your wedding?"

Anna shook her head. "I haven’t had a chance to talk to him yet. But I have something I need to tell you."

"You don’t need to say anymore, Anna. I forgive you.”

Anna looked into his kind, hazel eyes as she breathed a prayer for strength. "There is more to say. That afternoon in the barn…I’m pregnant."

Seth stumbled backward, shock pinning him against the barn door. His chest constricted while a mixture of emotions made it hard for him to breathe. The only thing he knew was that he loved her, but if she didn't return that love even now, he knew it would crush him like the weight of a horse sitting on his chest.

Anna suppressed the urge to comfort him. He was not handling the news well, and she could tell he was trying hard to accept it.

"It wasn't right what I put you through," Anna continued. "I'm sorry. I shouldn't have thought that I could marry a man who isn't the father of my baby."

Seth looked at her. "But isn't that exactly what you were expecting Maddie to do?"

Anna's eyes filled with fresh tears. "Yes it was. But that's only because she doesn't love her baby's father."

Seth finally pulled her into his arms, hope in his heart. "Are you saying you love me?"

"I think I've always loved you."

Seth was confused. "What do you mean *always*?"

"Well, I loved Nathan when we were children, but as we grew older, I began to love you differently. All Nathan and I had in common was quilting. He and I are the best of friends, but nothing more. I hadn't realized it before, but all the time I've spent with you made me fall deeply in love with you, and now I know what *real* love is. The kind of love you need to hold a life-long relationship together. A marriage."

Seth couldn't help but smile. "Does this mean you will marry me?"

Anna giggled. "Does this mean you are asking—again?"

Seth kissed her softly. "*Jah,* I am," he said between kisses.

Anna leaned into his kiss, feeling far more blessed than she ever thought she could be.

Chapter 12

Nathan stacked another wedge of firewood against his chest as he balanced the load with one arm. He'd gotten back to the house later than he'd expected, and he worried that Maddie could be sleeping. The house was dark when he'd pulled his truck into the driveway. After he'd done his chores at home, he had tried his best to locate Anna, but he had been unsuccessful. He'd waited around for Anna, hoping she would show up at her parent's house, but she hadn't even at this late hour. He had wanted to get their much-needed talk over with before he saw Maddie again. Now it didn't matter because Maddie was obviously sleeping, but he still had no closure with Anna, and that bothered him.

Nathan looked up at the dark windows of the house as he walked toward the back door, carrying the load of firewood in his arms. Now he would have to stack the firewood quietly in the house so as not to disturb Maddie. Turning the key in the lock of the kitchen door, he crept inside cautiously in case Maddie was roaming around the house. He did not want to startle her. He feared that knocking on the door would wake her if she was sleeping, so he opted to let himself in. After setting the wood near the hearth, he grabbed the poker and stirred the few remaining coals at the bottom of the grate. The glow of the embers and the crackle of the coals filled the room with bits of sound and light. He stacked splices of wood in a triangle, hoping that the remaining embers would spark the wedges.

While he waited for the wood to catch fire, Nathan crept quietly down the hall and stopped in the doorway of the room where Maddie lay sleeping. He entered the room, unable to resist the opportunity to admire her. As he drew closer, he could see her shivering beneath the light blanket that covered her. Grabbing a heavy quilt from the armoire shelf, Nathan unfolded it and gently draped it over her. He then pulled their butterfly quilt that was folded at the foot of the bed and placed it over the top of her and tucked it gently around her. He resisted the urge to brush aside the lock of golden hair that had fallen across her ivory cheek. Instead, he watched the rise and fall of her breath until she calmed under the warmth of the quilts. The strong urge to take care of her surprised him. He knew he cared for her, but he had put it out of his mind for so long, he'd become immune to her needs. Now she depended on him, and he would not let her down in this uncertain trial she faced.

Feeling exhausted, Nathan lowered himself into the chair near the window to wait for the fire in the sitting room to bring its warmth to the bedroom where Maddie slept soundly despite the deep chill in the air.

It wasn't long before Nathan's heavy eyelids drifted closed.

Maddie's eyes fluttered open a few times before she was able to focus on the silhouette that resembled Nate sitting in the chair beside the bed. Early morning moonlight shone through the sheer curtains, illuminating his handsome face just enough for Maddie to recognize him. The sky had begun to lighten, and the sun would probably be up within the hour.

But what was Nate doing there?

She poked her face out from under the covers and sniffed the air, noting the light scent of burning pine logs. Tiring of waiting on Nate to bring in the wood for the fire, she had gone to bed. It was obvious he had come while she was sleeping.

But why had he stayed by her side through the night?

Maddie pushed at the heavy quilts piled upon the bed that covered her, realizing Nate must have put them there. She smiled just thinking about it. She loved the thought of being taken care of by Nate, but she hoped he wasn't doing it out of obligation. She could not deny her heart's desire, for she was truly in love with him.

She prayed he could someday love her in return.

Chapter 13

Anna dreaded her meeting with Nathan, but it was the last bit of shocking news she had yet to deliver. This meeting would be harder than her meeting with Seth, for she didn't want to hurt Nathan. They had been friends most of their lives, and she wanted him to be as happy as she was, if that was possible.

If not for the strength that Seth had in backing her decision, she would probably be crumbling right now. Anna shoved her hands in the pockets of her wool coat to keep them from shaking. It surprised her that she shook more from nerves than from the cold. She was not prepared for what she was about to do, but it was inevitable. The child she carried depended on her to grow up and do the right thing, no matter how painful it was going to be for her. God had blessed her even in the midst of her disobedience, and she was determined to make things right with God for the sake of her child.

Letting go of her childhood friend was going to be one of the hardest things she could ever imagine, but she prayed that in time, Nathan would forgive her and they could go back to being friends. It was all they'd ever had aside from a silly childhood promise to remain together for the rest of their lives. They'd been foolish children to say the least, making a promise like that and expecting to live up to it.

It was simply not meant to be.

God had other plans for both of them, and it didn't involve the two of them getting married, in spite of their promise.

It was just not going to happen no matter how much they tried to keep it from falling apart.

Their love had been borne of a silly schoolyard promise and one innocent kiss.

Nothing more.

She prayed that Nathan would not obligate her to that promise in light of her present condition. She had betrayed his trust, that much was true, but there was no way around the reality of the love she and Seth had.

Taking a deep breath, Anna walked into the quilt shop where she knew Nathan would be. As she pushed open the door, the jingling of the bells on the door grated on her nerves. Her eyes scanned the shop, noting that Nathan and Maddie were working closely in the back. They were completing the final stitches of Ida Miller's wedding quilt, and Anna knew the over-zealous bride-to-be would be in to pick it up this afternoon.

Anna couldn't help but admire how well the two of them worked together. If she didn't know better, she might think that the two of them were better suited for one another than she and Nathan had been. They both seemed so happy, and they hadn't even noticed she'd walked into the shop. She stood still for a moment and watched the two of them work together.

They fit.

There was no denying it.

Anna cleared her throat, causing their gazes to lurch toward her. Nathan stood up abruptly and walked toward her, seriousness clouding his blue eyes.

Anna locked her gaze upon Nathan's, the anticipation of their discussion was almost too much to bear. She breathed a prayer that he would understand her sudden departure from his house. She was certain Maddie had broken the news to him by now. She detected from his expression that he already knew.

Maddie brushed by them nervously, excusing herself, as she grabbed her heavy coat and exited the shop. Anna watched Nathan, whose expression fell at Maddie's announcement.

It was obvious to Anna that he cared a great deal for Maddie, and that lightened the load weighing on her mind a little.

Chapter 14

Nathan's talk with Anna went better than he'd expected. He'd originally wondered if ending their long-time relationship would have an adverse effect on either of them, but surprisingly, they'd managed to salvage their friendship. Initially, he felt a little betrayed, but he could hardly hold her to a higher standard than he had for himself. After all, he'd fallen in love with Maddie around the same time.

Besides, Nathan would never begrudge Anna happiness, and if his cousin loved her, then he was happy for her. Finding out that she was with child was a bit of a shock, but he supposed it had been a surprise for the two of them as well. An impromptu wedding would be expected for the two of them, and that left Nathan free to pursue Maddie.

The thought of marrying Maddie both terrified and excited him. His only real fear where Maddie was concerned was to avoid rejection. He loved her, but he had no real way of knowing if she felt anything more than friendship for him the same way Anna had. Nathan had no interest in getting involved in another relationship that didn't go any farther than friendship. He was in love, and he didn't want to be hurt again. But by the same token, he didn't want to hurt Maddie in any way either. She'd been hurt enough, and he hoped his proposal would not add to her present grief.

All he wanted to do was to ease her pain and take care of her. He didn't want her to struggle through raising her child alone the way his birth mother had. They'd had a good enough life, him and his mom, but it would have been so much better if he'd had a father during those first seven years. His dad had more than made up for his absence during those first years, but Nathan had learned the importance of God's plan for having two parents raising their children—even for those who can't be together always. He knew that the quality of time was much more important sometimes than the quantity.

Nathan waited for Grandpa John to exit the house so they could talk in the barn without being overheard. It wasn't that he was keeping secrets from Grandma Nellie, but this was something he just needed his grandpa for. No one else understood him the way his grandpa did, and he needed some good, sound advice from the man.

When Grandpa John finally left the house, the two of them stepped into the barn. He'd called ahead to make certain that his grandpa would have time for him. The man was his only remaining tie to his birth mother; and for that, Nathan valued his relationship with him.

"By the look on your face, I'd say you look mighty upset about something," his grandpa said as they entered the warm barn.

"Anna broke it off with me and is marrying Seth," Nathan blurted out.

There was no point in repeating Anna's misfortune, for he'd been taught not to gossip.

His grandpa looked at him seriously. "I suppose that would upset me too. What do you aim to do about that?"

"Nothing," Nathan said. "I'm not upset over that."

John sat down on the stool he kept in front of his work bench. "Something has your feathers in a ruffle. What is it?"

Nathan felt like a fool for what he was about to say, but he *had* to tell *someone,* and he knew Grandpa would keep his confidence without judging him.

"It's Maddie," Nathan finally said. "I'm in love with her."

John chuckled. "I can't keep up with you young'uns anymore. Isn't she the pregnant girl living in your house?"

Nathan wanted to reveal Anna's secret pregnancy too, but he held his tongue. "Yes she is pregnant, but I don't care. I love her and I want to take care of her."

"Would you be making this decision if Anna hadn't broken things off with you?" John asked.

Nathan didn't have to give it a second thought. He'd been thinking about it for many months and had even run through different scenarios where *he* could be the one to break things off with Anna. He hadn't wanted to marry her for a long while, though he'd been willing to out of obligation. He wanted to marry Maddie because he truly loved her—not because he felt obligated the way he had with Anna.

"Anna and I never had anything stronger than friendship. I actually *love* Maddie, and I want to marry her if she'll have me."

Grandpa John smiled knowingly. "God gave me a second chance in life with your Grandma Nellie, and second chances don't often come around. So grab that second chance with Maddie. I'm behind you one hundred percent."

Nathan felt relief wash over him. He knew that his grandpa understood and supported his decision, and that meant everything to him at this unsure time.

The only thing he was certain of anymore was that he loved Maddie, and he intended to marry her.

Chapter 15

Nathan tip-toed into the house with a second load of firewood, trying not to disturb Maddie from her afternoon nap. She'd worked hard all week at the quilt shop, and being Sunday, she was overdue for some rest. He'd just set down the freshly cut pieces when he heard a car pull into the driveway. Looking up through the sitting room window, he wondered why the well-groomed man had pulled his bright red sports car into *his* driveway.

Nathan opened the door to find the young guy about his age peering into the windows of his truck and examining the logo for the quilt shop that he'd had painted on the side for advertising. He stepped off the porch to greet the stranger with a curious inquiry.

"Can I help you with something?" Nathan asked.

Running his hand over his dark, wavy hair, the man's gaze met Nathan's with a scowl. "I'm looking for Maddie Hayes. I was told she was staying here with some Amish dude."

Nathan tried not to let the guy's snarl when he said the word "Amish" bother him.

"I'm the Amish *dude*. What do you want with Maddie?"

The guy chuckled as he looked Nathan up and down. "You don't look Amish—except for that funny hat," he teased.

Nathan was tempted to rip the black, felt hat from his head and throw it at the disrespectful stranger, but he held his temper. "You didn't tell me what you want with Maddie."

The stranger took an aggressive step forward. "That's none of your business. It's between me and Maddie."

Nathan stood his ground. "The fact that you're on my property makes it my business."

He took another step toward Nathan. "Look here, Amish boy," he began.

The term grated on Nathan's nerves. It had become a *cute* term of endearment from Maddie's lips, but he was done letting this college boy disrespect him on his own property.

"I ain't leaving here until I see for myself if that girl is really pregnant with my kid," the stranger concluded.

So this was the one who'd hurt Maddie and then left her to fend for herself. Nathan wanted nothing more than to tell the guy she wasn't pregnant so he would leave. But as much as it pained him to give in to this intruder, it wasn't up to him. It was up to Maddie if she wanted to see him or not.

"Wait here," Nathan said reluctantly. "I'll see if she wants to see you."

"She'll see me!" he said arrogantly.

Nathan turned at his comment before walking into the small house that Maddie occupied alone.

"What's your name?"

Leaning against his car, he smirked at Nathan. "My name is Robert Wellington the Third."

"Of course it is," Nathan muttered under his breath. He knew Robert's type very well. Wealthy, spoiled, and arrogant, yet he lacked manners and respect.

Opening the kitchen door, Nathan dreaded telling Maddie of her visitor, no matter how much he wished he didn't have to.

Chapter 16

Nathan hated to wake Maddie from her sweet slumber, but the sooner she told Robert to leave, the better he would feel.

He walked lightly through the small house until he reached the open door of the bedroom where Maddie slept soundly—*his* bedroom. Leaning against the doorway, he couldn't help but give in to the thought of what life would be like if Maddie were to marry him.

Reality told him that the man waiting just outside for her could change those plans. It's funny that Nathan had never even given a second thought to the father of the baby Maddie carried.

To Nathan, it was Maddie's burden—a burden he wanted very much to turn into a blessing for the two of them. His plan had not taken into consideration Robert as the third party in the equation. But he'd shown up, nonetheless, and made his claim to the child. Would he make his claim on Maddie too?

Nathan feared that the most. He knew he could handle having Robert in their lives as a "weekend daddy", but to have him there permanently would leave Nathan out of the picture altogether, and he didn't like that scenario.

Watching Maddie sleep so soundly in his bed filled Nathan with a sense of pride as her protector. Once he woke her up, reality would take over, and this moment that belonged only to him could possibly slip away permanently. All because of the man who stood outside waiting to claim his family—the family Nathan desired more than his next breath.

Knowing he couldn't make excuses for the time he was wasting, Nathan walked quietly toward the bed and placed a gentle hand on Maddie's foot so as not to startle her. She stirred slightly, but her eyes remained closed.

Leaning down to whisper in her ear, Nathan was met by Maddie's arms swinging around his neck. She brushed her cheek lightly against his and sighed quietly. Nathan couldn't help but smooth back wisps of hair that fell across her eyes, hoping it would wake her a little more.

The temptation to press his lips to hers was almost unbearable for him, but he wasn't going to take advantage of her when she was sleeping.

She sighed and pulled him closer. "I love you," she whispered.

Nathan's heart raced as his mind tried to grasp a coherent thought. He cradled her head between his hands, cupping her cheeks, willing her to open her eyes so he could kiss her with good conscience. He loved her so much it nearly brought tears to his eyes.

Maddie's eye lashes fluttered until she focused on Nate. She wasn't dreaming. He was holding her, ready to kiss her just the way she'd imagined. She felt the weight of the quilts over her, but her arms were freely wrapped around Nate's neck, and his warm breath tickled her cheek.

Nathan peered into Maddie's eyes. He wanted to kiss her so much his heart ached.

But not like this.

Not with her baby's father waiting for her and expecting to claim his family—the family Nathan had no right to claim as his own no matter how much he wanted to.

Chapter 17

Maddie felt her heart quicken at the thought of seeing Robert again. She had been foolish to become so infatuated with him because of his good looks. It was that attraction that had gotten her into trouble. Her attraction to his looks had made him seem ugly afterward because of the man he'd turned out to be. She'd learned a hard lesson that outward beauty was not as important as what is in a man's heart.

Maddie sighed, unable to get past the unhappy look on Nathan's face when he'd told her about Robert's unannounced visit. His irritation with the situation had not gone unnoticed. When he'd said it, she could tell he was searching her eyes for a sign that she would reject his visit, but she felt compelled to know why he'd shown up after so many months had passed. Did she even want to see Robert? Was she ready to face him?

She had fallen in love with Nate at a time when she'd thought he could never return that love because of his commitment to Anna. Now that their relationship had abruptly ended, she held out hope for something beyond friendship with Nate and wanted nothing more to do with Robert, who'd turned his back on her. But how could she get Nate to see that? The hurtful look in his eyes had all but broken her heart. She did not want to hurt him, but she felt she owed it to her unborn child to hear what Robert had to say. If he wanted the opportunity to be a father to his child, she couldn't very well deny him that. But at what cost? Would his presence cost her the slim chance she had with Nate?

Maddie rubbed the sleep from her eyes as she threw a black cape over the plain blue dress she and Anna had sewn. Putting a hand to the back of her head, she pushed a few pins back in her hair that lay twisted at the nape of her neck.

Her mind drifted to the pleasant way in which Nate had woken her up. Disappointment surged through her as she struggled to understand why Nate hadn't kissed her. She'd wanted him to kiss her more than anything, but he'd held back. He'd come so close to kissing her, but then his demeanor had suddenly changed when he'd announced that Robert was outside waiting for her. He had sounded almost cold when he'd said it, and that upset and confused Maddie.

It was obvious to Maddie that Nate was upset by Robert's unexpected visit. To be honest, she wasn't too thrilled about it either. Nate's change in attitude had been abrupt to say the least, but Maddie tried not to read too much into it.

Outside, where Robert waited for her, Maddie stole a glance at him from the bedroom window. He was just as handsome as she'd remembered.

Be strong, she told herself. *He's not good for us.*

Maddie ran a hand over her abdomen at the light flutter she felt. It was *his* child, but how could she tell him tactfully that she didn't wish to have him in their lives? He hadn't had any trouble hurting her after she'd given up her virtue at his whims, but that didn't mean she was going to stoop to being the same kind of person he was. She had more respect for others than that, and it just wasn't part of her personality to be cruel—no matter what he'd done. True, he didn't deserve her kindness, but she would remain sincere to her new faith—the faith that had brought Nate into her life.

Chapter 18

Nathan stood at the entrance of the barn trying hard not to listen to Maddie's conversation. Deep down he meant to eavesdrop, but he wished he wasn't hearing what he was. The bits of conversation he overheard were strained at best, but that didn't ease his feelings of jealousy. Nathan tried to play it cool, but he was too tempted to throw that smooth-talking, rich snob off his property.

The only thing holding him back was that he knew Maddie had the right to make her own decision as to how to resolve her dilemma. It wasn't that he didn't trust Maddie to make the right decision; he didn't believe he could trust Robert not to hurt her again. So, he stood by, watching and listening, to ensure her safety. When the subject of marriage came up, Nathan's heart dropped to his feet.

"I will have to give that some thought," Maddie said to Robert. "I will give you my decision tomorrow."

What does she mean? Nathan asked himself. *Does she really intend to consider his half-hearted proposal? He doesn't love her—I do!*

Nathan witnessed Robert's attempt to hug Maddie, and her rigidness that made him back away from her.

Good girl, Nathan whispered under his breath.

Stealing a glance in her direction, his heart went out to her. The distraught look in her eyes was more than he could take. It took all the restraint he could muster to keep from rushing to her side and rescuing her from having to deal with Robert. He could tell by her body language that she didn't want anything more to do with him—so why had she agreed to think about it? Was it possible he was seeing his own agenda in her expression? If he was mistaken, his interference could cost him their friendship.

Against his better judgment, Nathan walked into the barn allowing the two of them some privacy.

Once he was out of the cold, he tried his best to occupy his mind with menial tasks, but even his horse, Duke, couldn't bring him out of his stupor. All he could think about was Maddie, and he worried that she might need him. Then it occurred to him that she may not need him at all, and that scared him more than the possibility of her marrying Robert.

He momentarily wondered if he should risk everything and tell her how he felt. He didn't want to cause her more confusion, but he wasn't certain he could just step aside and watch her marry Robert. Telling her posed the risk of hurting her, and he couldn't do that to her. Hurting her was just not an option for him the way it had been for Robert.

Chapter 19

"I didn't exactly mean it like that, Maddie," Robert said, crossing his arms in front of him.

"Are you taking back the proposal?" she asked.

"You don't really think I want to marry you, do you?" he asked with a smirk.

Humiliation and anger filled Maddie's thoughts. "Then why did you ask me?"

Robert shrugged. "My father doesn't want a family scandal."

Maddie was fuming.

She couldn't even look at him for fear she would be too tempted to slap him across his smug face.

"So you really only came over here to pay for my silence?"

Robert nodded casually. "Pretty much."

"I don't want your money! I don't want a single thing from you!" Maddie said through gritted teeth.

"I don't understand why you're getting so upset. We had a fun night together—that's all. Did you think I was going to fall in love with you?"

"Maybe in time…"

He was quick to interrupt her.

"That just isn't going to happen little cheerleader—well, I suppose you aren't a cheerleader anymore," Robert said with a hard chuckle.

Maddie couldn't think straight. Why was she getting so upset with this arrogant man who was practically a stranger to her? She didn't love him anymore than he loved her. Still, the humiliation of being rejected in her current state had caused her to become emotional.

"I want you to leave, Robert, and never look back. As far as I'm concerned, this child is not yours. I won't hold you responsible—for anything."

"I don't have a problem going back home and telling my father that I'm not the one who knocked you up."

Maddie cringed at his statement. He was too quick to dismiss his part in the conception. But more than that, he was not a man she would ever consider if he could walk away from her that easily.

She would rather raise her child alone than to force a man who wanted nothing to do with responsibility to take on the burden.

Her thoughts turned to Nate.

She was truly on her own in this.

The only thing left for her to do was to let Nate off the hook and leave his home before he felt obligated to help her any more than he already had.

Chapter 20

"Do you intend to marry Robert?" Nate asked Maddie as he set down his second load of firewood. He felt a drop of sweat trickle down the tense muscles of his back. He wasn't certain he was prepared for her answer, especially if the outcome was not in his favor.

Maddie paused to look at Nate thoughtfully. She loved him, but she still felt the uncertainty of what his role was in her life. His actions indicated he loved her, but she didn't dare hope for such a thing. She felt the weight of his indecision crushing her heart, and she tried not to think about his feelings for her. She had to face the fact that he may never return her love for him, and that terrified her. She couldn't allow her heart to continue to get caught up in him if he would not return the love she felt for him.

It would surely destroy her.

The crackle from the fireplace served as a cushion between them, and the warmth of the fire kept her from shaking more than she already was. Could she bear it if he never told her he loved her? It wasn't enough that she felt love from every gesture he directed toward her—she *needed* to hear him say the words. If he wasn't willing to articulate the emotional exchange, she would resolve her hope for a future with him by her side.

Her feelings would fade to nothing where she would bury them deep within her heart and never allow them freedom again. She would not risk her heart for nothing, and she certainly could not endure anymore rejection.

Maddie gazed into the fire, not wanting to admit the humiliation of Robert's empty proposal.

"I suppose I will consider marrying Robert—unless you can give me a reason not to."

She knew she risked everything with that statement, but she no longer wished to waste time with playing it safe.

Nathan stared at her profile. The amber glow from the firelight flickered over her ivory skin, giving her a sun-kissed radiance. The curve of her pregnancy added to her natural beauty, making it nearly impossible to resist the urge to pull her into his arms. He wanted to kiss her more than he wanted to take his next breath. He fought to remember when he'd fallen so deeply in love with her, but none of that mattered now. She would marry Robert, and Nathan would have to let her go, no matter how right they were for one another.

He struggled with the words to say to her, but everything that entered his mind was selfish. Though the temptation to claim the child as his own and send Robert on his way was strong, he didn't have the right to stand between a man and his child. It wasn't his place to decide that—it was Maddie's. The only moral answer to Maddie's question was a resounding negative one. The only reason he could give her was that he loved her, and he feared it would never be enough.

"I'm sorry, Maddie, I can't."

Maddie's throat constricted and her chest heaved with sobs that she refused to release in front of Nate. She ran to the bathroom to escape his scrutiny.

She would not let him see her cry.

How could she have been so foolish to think that Nate could love her when she was carrying another man's child?

He didn't want her either.

Slamming the bathroom door behind her, she sank to the floor and let go of her emotions quietly.

Chapter 21

Nathan struggled as he watched Maddie packing her few belongings. But as she gestured toward the butterfly quilt, he couldn't continue to watch her removing herself from his life. His love for her would have to be enough to stop her from leaving—wouldn't it?

He certainly hoped it was so.

Stepping forward, he placed his hand on hers to stop her from removing the quilt that had become part of his home. It was the only thing that was a part of the two of them that made any sense to him. If he allowed her to remove it from his bed, he feared losing her forever.

"I understand if you want me to leave it for you," she whispered, his hand still preventing her from tearing it from the bed.

Nathan swallowed his fear.

It was now or never.

"I want you to leave it for *you*," he offered gently.

Maddie caught his serious expression, trying to comprehend the meaning behind his words.

"I couldn't bear to see that quilt leave my house any more than I could stand it if *you* left," he said.

Maddie felt confusion gripping her heart. Was she about to have her heart's desire, or would he continue to keep his feelings silent?

"You want me to…stay?" she barely whispered.

"More than ever," he admitted with a smile so wide his dimples sent shivers through her.

"I would much rather stay with you," Maddie conceded, letting out the breath she'd been holding in.

"What about the fact that I'm Amish?" Nathan asked.

It didn't matter to Nathan that he wasn't Amish by blood relation, because to him, he would always be Amish because of his mother. He wanted to be sure that Maddie would be able to live with that.

"Don't you know by now that I love you, Amish boy?" Maddie said with a giggle.

Nathan smiled as he pulled her into his arms. "I'm glad to hear that, because I love you too."

Maddie felt the weight of anticipation escape her in one smooth breath. They were the most wonderful words that could ever tickle her ears.

Nathan pressed his lips to hers, kissing her with all the built-up energy he'd been pushing aside for too long. Tucking his arm around her waist, he pulled her so close that only his racing heart stood between them. Her heart's rhythm echoed his own as he deepened the kiss, unwilling to let her go just yet. Warmth coursed through her as she felt herself fall into a mesmerizing state of total bliss. She had loved this man so much it hurt, but now, as he kissed her, all that pain turned to pure joy.

"I love you so much I want you to be my *fraa*," Nate declared.

Maddie looked at him curiously. "*Fraa*? What is that?"

Nathan kissed her again. "If you are going to be married to an Amish man, you better learn the language."

"Married? Did you just ask me to marry you?" She was almost too afraid to ask the question.

Nathan smiled brightly. "*Jah*, I believe I did."

Maddie threw her arms around his neck and kissed him. "I would love to be your *fraa,*" she said.

Nathan scooped her up and twirled her around, feeling like the happiest man in the world.

THE END

DON'T MISS THESE OTHER BOXED SETS!

Amish Wildflowers FREE on

Kindle Unlimited

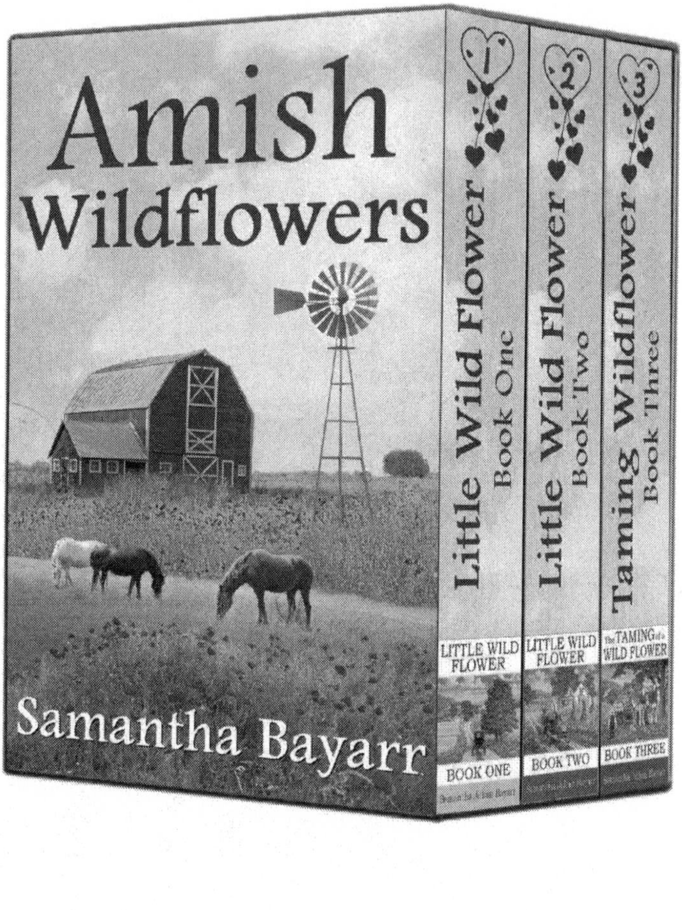